EDITOR: MARTIN WINDROW

 MEN-AT-ARMS SERIES | 96

ARTILLERY EQUIPMENTS OF THE NAPOLEONIC WARS

Text by
TERENCE WISE
Colour plates by
RICHARD HOOK

D1421372

Published in 1979 by
Osprey Publishing Ltd
Member company of the George Philip Group
59 Grosvenor Street, London W1X 9DA
© Copyright 1979 Osprey Publishing Ltd
Reprinted 1980, 1982, 1983, 1984, 1985
1986, 1987 (twice), 1988, 1989, 1991

ISBN 0 85045 336 4

Filmset in Great Britain
Printed in Hong Kong through Bookbuilders Ltd

Acknowledgements
The author wishes to thank the following people,
who have kindly assisted his research by advice,
translation, or the loan of books or original material
from their files: Stephen Crich, Fred Feather, John
Hickman, Peter Hofschröer, J. D. Perkins, Otto
von Pivka, Norman Swales and Alan Hansford
Waters for reference to material on organization from
his unpublished manuscript 'Ça Ira'. The author also
wishes to thank Robert Wilkinson-Latham for
making available from his collection many of the
illustrations in this book.

Author's Note
The term 'battery' was not in common use until the
end of the period covered by this book, a battery
being an emplacement occupied by artillery.
However, since an artillery company was the
strength normally employed in a battery the two
terms became synonymous. In this text I have used
'battery' where necessary, for both convenience
and clarity.

The Equipments

At the start of the French Revolutionary Wars the artillery corps of most European armies were equipped with a mixture of 3pdr., 6pdr. and 12pdr. field guns, the calibre being measured by the weight of the roundshot fired. The exceptions were France, Spain and Bavaria, which followed a standardized 4pdr., 8pdr. and 12pdr. system introduced in France by Jean Baptiste de Gribeauval, Inspector General of Artillery from 1776. However, it should be noted that weights were not standardized in the 18th or early 19th centuries, and a glance at the accompanying Table A will show that the French 8pdr. was in fact 8.8 English pounds so that, with the variation in calibres experienced in casting at this date, there was not a great difference between the French 8pdr. and the 9pdr. subsequently re-adopted by the British artillery.

Britain had 4.4in. and 5.5in. field howitzers; France had 6in. and 8in. ones; and Prussia, Russia, Denmark and Austria used mainly 7pdrs.

and 10pdrs., this last designation being an archaic one based on the weight of a stone projectile which could have fitted their bore. The 7pdr. howitzer had a bore of 5.7 inches, as opposed to the British 5.5-inch bore; the 10pdr. was roughly equal to the French 6-inch bore.

The system of light and manoeuvrable 3pdr., 6pdr. and 12pdr. field guns had been introduced by Austria at the beginning of the Seven Years War and had proved so successful that the other powers had soon copied it. Frederick the Great of Prussia had gone one further by developing an ultra-light 6pdr. 'galloper' gun. Galloper guns had been employed with the cavalry arm for some time, but this new piece was soon adopted by most European countries and eventually led to the development of the distinct horse artillery. These formations employed a lighter piece of the existing calibre, sacrificing weight and impact of projectile, and to some degree range, in the interests of speed. Thus 'light' 6pdrs. and 'light' field howitzers were cast by most countries in addition to their other pieces.

There was one other type of artillery introduced

TABLE A: Comparative Weights

Variations in the weights and measures used throughout Europe in the Napoleonic period should be taken into account when considering the artillery equipments of the day. The following figures are taken from *A Universal Military Dictionary, in English and French* by Charles James, London, 1816. The 100lbs. of England, Scotland and Ireland were equal to:

lbs.	oz.	Country/Province	lbs.	oz.	Country/Province
91	8	Amsterdam	137	4	Genoa
96	8	Antwerp/Brabant	132	11	Leghorn
96	5	Liège	153	11	Milan
91	8	Paris	152	0	Venice
88	0	Rouen	154	10	Naples
106	0	Lyons	104	13	Portugal
107	11	Toulouse/Languedoc	112	8	Spain: *but*
113	0	Marseilles/Provence	97	0	Seville, Cadiz
81	7	Geneva	112	$\frac{2}{3}$	Russia
89	7	Frankfurt	107	0	Sweden
93	5	Hamburg	89	$\frac{1}{2}$	Denmark

12pdr. gun, carriage and limber of Swedish design, c.1790, showing method of limbering and type of limber in general use in most European armies during the 1792–1815 period. The wooden wedge under the end of the barrel was replaced by an elevating screw by *circa* 1805 at latest. (Kungl. Armemuseum, Stockholm)

during the period covered by this book, and unique to Britain: rocketry. However, rocketry consists of ammunition without a firing piece, or 'ammunition without ordnance, it is the soul of artillery without the body', as its inventor termed it, and therefore it is covered under the heading of Ammunition.

★   ★   ★

In the first half of the 18th century the French had been the European leaders in artillery, possessing the only standardized range of pieces, known as the de Vallière system. These pieces, ranging from 4pdrs. to 24pdrs., were sturdy but extremely heavy. At the beginning of the Seven Years War, Austria seized the lead by introducing new light field pieces—the 3pdr., 6pdr. and 12pdr. guns—and some excellent light howitzers. Other powers adopted this new system (the French

copied the field howitzer as late as 1803), though the Prussians, unable to afford a completely new range of artillery, adopted only the light 6pdr. and light 12pdr.

Gribeauval served with the Austrian artillery from 1756–62, and when he returned to France he was called upon to reorganize the French artillery. His proposed reforms were bitterly opposed for some years, the opposition being led by de Vallière's son, and could not be implemented until 1776; but from then until his death in 1789 he established a system which was to revolutionize the artillery of Europe and make possible the highly efficient field artillery of the Napoleonic Wars.

The Gribeauval system for the first time created a complete, unified range of artillery; not just the pieces but their carriages, limbers, ammunition wagons, and the tools to serve them. At the same time he divided artillery into four distinct types—field, siege, garrison and coastal—relegating all calibres above the 12pdr. to the last three categories in order to form a highly mobile field artillery.

His technical innovations included a reduction in windage (the difference between the calibre of the barrel and the diameter of the projectile, which had been as much as half an inch) and this made possible a reduction of the propellant charge without loss of range or impact. This in turn enabled pieces to be cast thinner and shorter, and their carriages could therefore be constructed shorter and narrower, creating much lighter equipments: Gribeauval's 12pdr., for example, was only half the weight of its predecessor.

French howitzer, Gribeauval system. Again, note handspike stowage, chains and brackets, and particularly the drag rope hooks on the axle washers, all for manhandling the piece in action. (Musée de l'Armée)

Austrian 3pdr. gun of the 18th century, which continued to be employed in the Austrian army throughout the Napoleonic Wars. Note stowage of tools, chains, and handspike brackets for manhandling the piece in action. (Ottenfeld)

But the most important factor of his system was standardization: carriages were, as far as possible, usable for several different weights of guns and even howitzers (although some howitzers had a slightly different carriage with a marginally shorter trail), and axles and wheels were interchangeable between carriages, limbers and ammunition caissons.

The characteristic carriage of the second half of the 18th century was of the so-called double-bracket type, formed from two wooden planks called cheeks or brackets, placed on edge almost parallel to each other (the gap narrowed slightly at the rear) and connected by four cross-pieces called transoms. These transoms were known, from front to rear of the carriage, as the breast, bed, centre and trail transoms. The bed and centre transoms were close together and over them was placed a board known as the bed: quoins or wedges rested on the bed to support the base ring of the barrel, and these could be adjusted to alter the elevation of the barrel.

The axle-tree was just behind the breast transom. Over the fore part of the axle-tree, on the top edges of the brackets, were the trunnion holes and capsquares, the latter being curved iron straps which fitted over the trunnions to hold them securely in the trunnion holes. The capsquares were usually hinged at one end and fastened by a pin at the other, but the heaviest pieces were often held by capsquares pinned at both ends.

In the trail transom was a metal-lined pintle hole for linkage to the limber. Also on the trail transom were four metal eye rings for handspikes, and there were two elongated metal brackets on the tops of the cheeks, near the cascable (the 'knob' on the central rear surface of the breech), for the same purpose. Gribeauval not only made these carriages lighter, reinforcing the much lighter construction with metal strapping, but also replaced the wooden axles with iron ones for greater strength. In addition, the carriage was fitted with hooks for drag ropes and for storage of rammers, sponges, handspikes, buckets and other such 'ready' equipment.

Gribeauval also reduced the limber to a light

French 8pdr. carriage and limber of the Gribeauval system. The ammunition chest is in position across the trail. (Musée de l'Empéri)

French ammunition caisson for horse artillery, with seat and handles for gunners, and spare wheel, limbered to the older type of ammunition-bearing limber. (Musée de l'Armée)

A-frame—an axle-tree and two wheels—with a pintle on top of the axle-tree to fit the corresponding hole in the trail transom of the gun carriage. The shafts formerly used for harnessing the draught-horses were replaced by a single pole, while the wheels had their diameter increased to four feet to give a better performance over rough ground.

The loss of the conventional ammunition limber was compensated for by a small 'ready supply' of ammunition carried in a metal-reinforced chest, placed between the brackets of the carriage, where it was supported by its carrying handles resting on the brackets. When the piece was in action this chest was either placed on the ground nearby or rested on the A-frame of the limber.

The bulk of the ammunition was carried in caissons, designed by Gribeauval to hold the new 'fixed' ammunition, i.e. projectile and propellant made up into one. The caisson was an eleven-foot-long, narrow-bodied wagon with a sloping lid hinged to open, the interior being divided into compartments for the assembled rounds. Powder and matches were also carried in the caisson, as were shovels and a pick (fastened to the sides), a detachable tool-box at the front, and a spare wheel (of the five-foot diameter used for gun carriage and caisson rear wheels) on the rear of the caisson. The front wheel unit had the four-foot diameter wheels and was identical to the limber unit in construction, so that the two were interchangeable. A light caisson was also produced (presumably for horse artillery use) only 7ft. 6in. long and without either spare wheel or tool-box. Caissons were allocated at the rate of two for each 4pdr., three for each 8pdr., and five for each 12pdr.

French horse artillery seems to have relied during the Napoleonic Wars on the older type of ammunition limber to some extent, while at its formation in 1791 it used the 'Wurst' wagon attributed to the Austrians, but possibly a French adaptation of the ordinary caisson. This consisted of a caisson with a flat lid padded to form a seat, foot boards added at each side, and a wooden

7

cross attached at front and rear. Crew members rode astride this seat, the front and rear men holding on to the crosses and the others holding on to each other. The '*Wurst*' caisson continued to be used by the Austrian horse artillery during the Napoleonic Wars, but not by the French.

The artillery of the other major powers was soon affected by the Gribeauval system: like all great advances its essence—standardization to provide interchangeability in the field—was simple. The influence of the Gribeauval system may be seen in the accompanying illustrations of the equipments of the various powers, but it can also be seen that they retained some national characteristics. The Prussians, Russians and Austrians, for example, adopted the simple A-frame limber but retained ammunition chests on the limber in addition to the trail chest, the

Austrians only for their heaviest pieces, the Russians for their light and medium pieces.

Russian ammunition caissons resembled the French ones, but came in short and long versions, the former having only two wheels and twin shafts for a single horse (sufficient for haulage when the caisson was empty), extra horses being harnessed ahead in single file when laden. The Austrians also used two sizes of caisson, a small two-wheeled, two-horse one for the 3pdr. and the 7pdr. howitzer, and larger, four-wheeled, four-horse ones for the 6pdrs. and 12pdrs.

Over the years the British adopted the essence of the Gribeauval system, with wheels of a uniform diameter and standardized patterns for the carriages of each calibre so that any one part might be replaced by the corresponding part from another carriage; but they did not, of

Prussian 6pdr. field gun, carriage and limber, again with both the traditional ammunition chest on the limber and the trail box. Note rods from limber wheels to traces: these are peculiar to Prussian and Russian limbers.

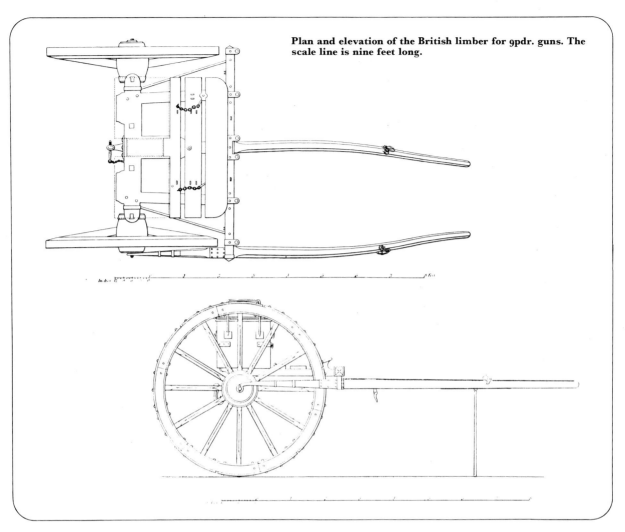

Plan and elevation of the British limber for 9pdr. guns. The scale line is nine feet long.

course, use the same calibre pieces as the French. Nor did the British adopt the single-pole limber and caisson, retaining the double-shaft ammunition limber and, until 1800, a long four-wheeled ammunition wagon resembling the more modern G.S. wagon. In 1800 this was abandoned in favour of a more manoeuvrable vehicle, a second limber without shafts simply being hooked up behind the draught limber and loaded with ammunition boxes. Ammunition and draught limbers were of the same construction, apart from the shafts, which on the rear limber were replaced by a short pole, and the only variation was in the dimensions of the boxes placed upon them, these boxes varying slightly in size according to the type of ammunition. Some, but not all, of these caissons carried a spare wheel at the rear.

The combination of limber and gun carriage, or limber and caisson, produced articulated four-wheeled vehicles capable of shifting considerable weights across country at good speeds, so that under normal conditions the artillery could keep up with the rest of the army. But despite Gribeauval's improvements, equipments were still far from light; the French 12pdr., for example, weighed almost two tons, and the 8pdr. and 12pdr. carriages had to have two sets of trunnion holes (this being the main difference from howitzer carriages, which had only one set) so that when on the move the heavy barrels could be carried in the rear holes to provide a better point of balance. This meant some delay when first coming into action, as the barrel of a 12pdr. weighed almost a ton.

Another disadvantage was that all gunners in the French Foot Artillery had to march on foot, instead of riding on the ammunition limber, as was still done to some extent under the British,

Austrian and Russian systems. The British limber seated two men and up to six more could ride on the ammunition caisson, though orders frequently prohibited this except in emergencies. On Russian and Austrian limbers the ammunition boxes could serve as seats for two gunners, and it appears that in the Russian Foot Artillery another gunner may have been seated on the trail of the gun, as was done in the Austrian horse artillery.

French artillery also seems to have been less manoeuvrable than the British artillery, perhaps the prime example being Waterloo, where the French had some difficulty in getting their 12pdrs. into position over the soft ground, whereas no British diarist mentions a similar problem for the 9pdr. (A 9pdr., modelled on the British piece, was introduced into the French Army shortly after the 1815 Restoration on the recommendation

of Marshal Marmont, himself a distinguished gunner.) Partly this may have been due to the extra weight of the 12pdr., but the introduction of the block trail into the British system in 1792 would also have been a factor, and this trail probably made the British artillery more manoeuvrable than the artillery of any other power.

The block trail field carriage was designed by Lieutenant-General Sir William Congreve (appointed Comptroller of the Royal Laboratory, Woolwich, in 1793) and consisted of two short brackets to house the piece, fitted to a single, solid wood trail of rectangular cross section. This considerably reduced the weight of the trail and also placed the centre of gravity for the whole equipment much further forward, thus lightening the trail even more, so that limbering and unlimbering could be done with ease, while one

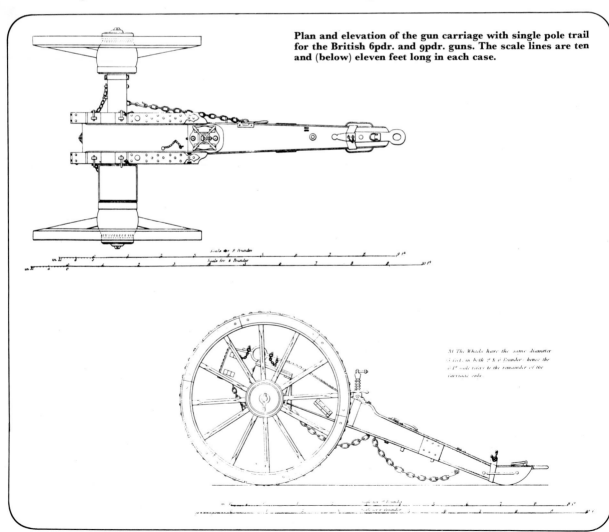

Plan and elevation of the gun carriage with single pole trail for the British 6pdr. and 9pdr. guns. The scale lines are ten and (below) eleven feet long in each case.

man (the gun commander) could alone traverse and aim the gun, thus speeding up the rate and accuracy of fire. The single trail also greatly increased the angle of lock possible, reducing the turning circle of the carriage when in draught, and generally gave greater mobility and speed in turning and manoeuvring.

The block trail was first introduced in 1792 for the 6pdr. gun and was later adopted for the 9pdr. when this was brought back into service. A block trail was designed for the 5.5in. howitzer but never manufactured, and these pieces used a bracket carriage with a very short trail throughout the Napoleonic Wars, the combination of a light carriage and relatively light piece producing a weapon which was as handy if not handier in action than the guns.

In addition to the ammunition caissons there were a number of other vehicles which had important rôles in every artillery company, carrying extra ammunition, spare wheels, gun carriages and axles, pickaxes, shovels, powder, artificers' tools, farriers' equipment and even mobile forges. Chief amongst these were the artillery park wagons, which formed a sort of 'B' echelon, carrying the reserve ammunition and spares; and the baggage wagons which accompanied each company, holding an assortment of spares and necessities. These wagons were simple box structures for the most part, four-wheeled, with iron

Austrian 6pdr. gun for horse artillery, with ammunition chest on trail covered to provide a seat for the gunners. The *kanonier* is wearing pre-1806 uniform. (Ottenfeld)

hoops to support their canvas tilts.

Another vehicle which accompanied each company was the two- or four-wheeled mobile forge. This consisted of a flat bed lined at one end with iron plate to take a fire, another iron plate set vertically near the centre of the bed to prevent the fire spreading, bellows at the rear of the bed, and a wooden trough for water. Boxes secured to the end nearest the team held an assortment of tools, and of course coal was also carried. The French four-wheeled forges utilized the standard

British 5.5in. howitzer, bracket carriage and limber.

limber for the front wheels and method of draught.

In the artillery park were a number of specialist vehicles. The block carriage or platform wagon was used to transport siege pieces which were too heavy to be moved on their own carriages, and consisted of two long beams laid lengthwise on two sets of wheels. It could carry two 8in. mortars with their wooden firing beds, and in the British service weighed just over a ton.

The gyn was a portable crane for lifting heavy pieces on and off their carriages, or setting mortars on their beds, and consisted of three sheerlegs and a lifting tackle with a number of handling blocks. There were two types of gyn in the British service, the largest weighing 12cwt, two quarters and 19½lbs with all the blocks, etc., and the smaller weighing 10cwt, two quarters and 4lbs.

The sling wagon was a four-wheeled vehicle with a rack and handle mounted in the centre, used to carry a mortar already mounted on its bed over short distances, i.e. from one firing position to another, the mortar being slung beneath the axle of the wagon. In the British service such vehicles weighed 31cwt and 23lbs. A smaller, two-wheeled version, weighing 16cwt, one quarter and 17lbs, was used to move mortar and bed separately.

French four-wheeled field forge with standard limber. (Musée de l'Armée)

The Teams

All vehicles had originally been drawn by animals harnessed in single file, and another major advance of the 18th century had been the harnessing of teams in pairs. The rear pair of draught animals in any team were harnessed to the limber by traces, and were known as wheelers. Their task was not only to hold and steady the limber by its pole or shafts, but also to steer it in the horizontal plane. Despite Gribeauval's reforms, the French limber wheels at this date remained four feet high while the end of the limber pole rose to about five feet, creating a difference of some two feet between the end of the pole and the line of traction (the axle-tree). The pulling of the rest of the team therefore tended to drag the end of the pole down, while the wheelers had to struggle to hold it up, and even the strongest wheelers did not last long as a consequence. The different wheel diameters in use in other artillery corps created the same problem.

All countries except Britain (and to a very limited extent Russia), which retained the shafts, used the single central pole of the Gribeauval system. (The British shafts were offset on the offside to make room for two wheelers.) The front ends of the pole or shafts were secured to the harness of the wheelers and the remaining pairs

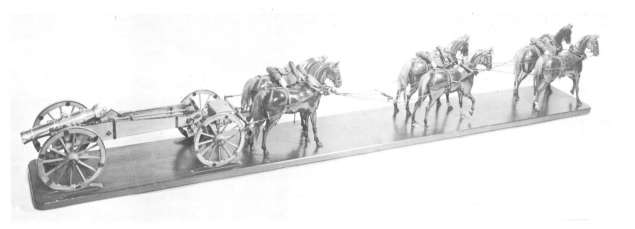

12pdr. gun, carriage, limber and fully harnessed team of the Russian 1805 system, illustrated by a model presented to the King of Sweden by Czar Nicholas I (1825–55). The harnessing system for Prussian artillery was similar. (Kungl. Armemuseum, Stockholm)

of the team were then attached to the end of the pole or shafts by harness and traces. The nearside horses were saddled and ridden by the drivers, who controlled the offside horses in each pair by a single rein and by pressing a short whip against that horse's neck.

In the British artillery the 6pdr. guns and light howitzers were normally pulled by teams of six horses, the 9pdrs. by teams of eight. (Four and six horses respectively in peacetime establishments, but this was usually insufficient for active service conditions.) Ammunition caissons, forges and spare wheel carriages were pulled by teams of six, all other wagons by teams of four: mules were sometimes used for the wagons.

In the French artillery the 4pdr. guns were most commonly pulled by teams of six horses and the 12pdrs. by teams of eight to twelve, depending on circumstances. The sources consulted avoid mentioning the 8pdr., but presumably teams of eight would normally have been sufficient.

The official figures for Austrian artillery show 3pdrs. drawn by teams of two, 6pdr. and 7pdr. howitzers by teams of four, and 12pdrs. by teams of six, but in the field larger teams were probably used, perhaps even double these figures. The caissons were drawn by two- and four-horse teams, as mentioned earlier, but there were in the artillery reserve caissons drawn by six-horse teams. Horse artillery pieces were drawn by six horses, with a two-horse caisson and four pack-horses carrying more ammunition.

The Russians used four horses for their lightest pieces and eight for the 12pdrs. and heaviest unicorns (a type of howitzer), though ten horses were used in bad conditions. Russian horses were small but had great strength and endurance, and the teams were well organized.

In the Prussian artillery six-horse teams were employed for caissons, 6pdr. guns and 7pdr. howitzers; eight-horse teams for 12pdrs.; and four-horse teams for supply and tool wagons, etc.

All these teams remained hooked in when in action, those of the caissons and limbers being held immediately to the rear of the guns (caissons were about twenty paces behind the guns), and thus exposed to enemy fire, while those of the other vehicles with the companies found some sort of cover a short distance to the rear. It would appear the horses pulling spare wheel carriages and even the baggage wagons were regarded as reserve horses for gun carriage and caisson teams.

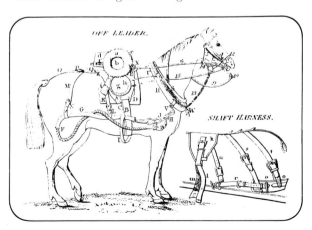

British offside leader horse with full detail of harness. The nearside horses had similar harness but with a saddle. Harness for the 'wheelers' is also shown. (Robert Wilkinson-Latham)

A system known as prolonge was sometimes employed to increase manoeuvrability over rough ground: this consisted of a long rope or chain lashing between team and gun. Pieces were also advanced by manhandling during battles, especially if supporting infantry attacks, and in these cases the drag ropes were used by the crews: in the Austrian artillery it was considered that a strong and fresh team of gunners and handlers could heave a field piece forward at a greater speed than marching infantry.

The Ammunition

Another improvement to the efficiency of artillery in the field was fixed or ready ammunition, that is projectile and propellant joined in one. Theoretically such ammunition was initially supposed to be reserved for rapid firing, but in practice gunners undoubtedly went for fixed ammunition every time—always provided it was available. Loose powder was still carried in the field, however, but its use was probably limited to mortars, which had to adjust the weight of individual charges in order to alter their range, being on a fixed elevation of 45°. The advantages of fixed ammunition were obvious: a greatly increased rate of fire, and reduced risk of premature explosion through loose powder lying about.

The correct weight of powder, usually calculated at about a quarter to a third the weight of a roundshot, and rather more than one-third the weight of canister, was contained in a bag, the mouth of which was secured by a string. The old fashioned wad was replaced by a 'sabot' or shoe of wood, usually elm or alder, which was equal in diameter to the gauge of the projectile, and dished to receive up to a quarter of the projectile. The projectile was most often secured to the sabot by two tinned iron straps, crossed over the top of the projectile and nailed to the sabot, though other methods were employed (see Plate A). Finally the sabot was inserted into the mouth of the powder bag and the string tied round a groove in the edge of the sabot or, as in the British artillery, nailed to the sabot with copper tacks. Two more strings were tied round the bag at the middle and top to keep it in the correct shape and to strengthen it.

Austrian near and offside horses with full harness.

Flannel or serge was used to make these bags, both materials being totally consumed on firing. The cloth was usually boiled in glue size to stiffen it and seal the weave before being made into bags: in the Austrian artillery a special paste was used instead and the bags were then painted with white oil paint. (British canister containers may have been painted red.)

Improvements were also made to the quality of the black powder, mainly by the establishment of government mills. The powder was a mixture of saltpetre, charcoal and sulphur, the exact proportions varying very little from country to country, yet British powder was considered by far the best. This was probably due entirely to the quality of the charcoal and saltpetre used. It was essential that the powder be completely consumed on firing, and it was the quality of the charcoal which affected the other ingredients in achieving this end: in Britain the charcoal had been made in closed containers since *circa* 1786, and was consequently greatly superior to that used by other countries.

Saltpetre was found naturally in tropical climates, but could be manufactured artificially in Europe: Britain, France, Prussia and Sweden had all established factories for this purpose during the 18th century. However, home-produced saltpetre cost four times as much as the imported product, and Britain therefore relied exclusively

TABLE C: Barrel Lengths; Barrel and Carriage Weights

Country	Piece	Barrel Length (inches)	Barrel Weight (pounds)	Barrel/Carriage Weight (pounds)
Austria	3pdr.	45	530	?
	6pdr.	$58\frac{1}{4}$	912	?
	12pdr.	75	1,790	?
	7pdr. how.	?	617	?
	10pdr. how.	?	1,676	?
Britain	3pdr.	42	280	784
	6pdr. HA	60	672	1,652
	6pdr. FA	84	1,372	2,624
	9pdr.	72	1,512	2,828
	5.5in. how. HA	$26\frac{3}{4}$	532	1,680
	5.5in. how. FA	33	1,120	2,548
France	4pdr.	63	637	2,091
	6pdr.	70	850	?
	8pdr.	79	1,286	2,137
	12pdr.	91	2,172	4,364
	6in. how.	28	701	2,596
Prussia	6pdr. HA	62	880	1,700
	6pdr. FA	?	1,455	2,615
	12pdr.	78	1,780	3,380
	7pdr. how. HA	36	500	1,630
	7pdr. how. FA	?	700	1,830
	10pdr. how.	$41\frac{1}{4}$	1,280	3,000
Russia	6pdr.	$63\frac{3}{4}$	?	?
	12pdr.	$77\frac{1}{2}$	?	?
	10pdr. how.	53	?	?
	20pdr. how.	$64\frac{1}{4}$	?	?

All weights and measurements in this unavoidably incomplete table are approximate, as they are translated from various national forms.

FA = foot artillery   HA = horse artillery

TABLE D: Colour Schemes

Gathered from various sources, these descriptions can only be general in some cases; equally, they should not be taken as absolutely rigid within any one country's artillery corps. The Napoleonic age had not yet seen the triumph of the centralized bureaucracy over the individual!

Country	Woodwork	Metal carriage fittings
Austria	Ochre	Black
Baden	Dark grey	,,
Bavaria	Light blue-grey	,,
England	Blue-grey	,,
France	Olive green*	,,
Hesse-Darmstadt	Mid-blue	,,
Naples	Light blue	,,
Prussia	Mid-blue	,,
Russia	Apple green	Polished
Saxony	Dark grey	Yellow
Sweden	Greenish-blue	Black
Wurttemberg	Natural wood	Yellow
Brunswick	Light blue (?)	Black
Italy	Grey (?)	,,
Westfalia	Green (?)	,,

(* = 2,500 grammes of yellow ochre to 30 grammes black)

Barrel colours

Brass/bronze barrels were polished in barracks but left dull in the field. Iron barrels were normally painted, to protect them from rust; this paint must have worn and burned off very quickly in an action, and the gunners must have spent many 'spare' hours cleaning and re-painting them. Black paint seems to have been quite common, but not universal. There is a reference to British barrels being painted with, apparently, a mixture of red and black, which would have given a very dark brown finish. (It may be significant that there are contemporary references to the guns of Royal Navy men-o'-war being painted chocolate brown on some occasions.) No rigid statement can be made as to the ratio of iron to bronze guns in use in any country. Bronze was favoured for the field pieces, having a better strength/weight ratio and lacking iron's brittleness, although prolonged firing over a period caused the barrels to droop and distort.

on the cheap yet fine-grade saltpetre from India. Britain ruled the seas, and the quality of French powder therefore suffered as a direct result of the Royal Navy's blockade. The quality of French gunpowder was particularly bad in 1814.

Three main types of projectile were fired by this powder: cannonball or roundshot, canister or case-shot, and common shell. The most important of these was roundshot, a solid iron ball in various diameters. It was used against targets at all ranges and depended for its effect on the velocity with which it struck the target. Therefore it was mainly fired from the long barrels of guns, which could produce the greatest muzzle velocity, though it was also used by howitzers to a small degree. The heavier the shot the greater its velocity, and a 12pdr. was therefore 50 per cent more effective than a 6pdr., although the difference in shot diameter was relatively small (French 6pdr. = 3.66in., 12pdr. = 4.60in.).

It was possible for enemy roundshot to be fired back, once the calibre had been checked, but a roundshot was too hot to handle on arrival and even when immobile had to be treated with respect. In 1814 France was reduced to relying to some extent on such scrap ammunition and this, combined with poor powder, affected both the range and accuracy of the French artillery.

Canister was used only at short range, by both guns and howitzers, and consisted of a thin tin cylinder, a little less in diameter than the calibre of the piece, with a wooden sabot bottom and an iron lid soldered on. (The Austrian canister had

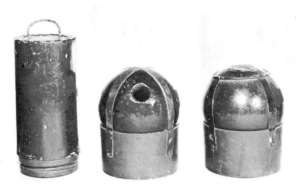

Canister, common shell (with fuze removed) and roundshot, illustrating wooden 'sabots' or shoes and methods of fixing projectile to sabot. Notice groove on canister sabot, to enable charge bag to be lashed on. (Kungl. Armemuseum, Stockholm)

an inch-thick sabot of wrought iron.) This tin was packed with balls to make up the weight of the projectile, and the cylinder held these balls together during its passage up the bore. Sawdust filled the spaces between the balls. As it left the confines of the barrel the pressure of the charge and the relaxation of the inward pressure of the barrel caused the cylinder to disintegrate so that the balls continued forward, splaying outwards to form a cone of death with a diameter of 32 feet at 100 yards, 64 feet at 200 yards, and 96 feet at 300 yards.

The number and size of the balls contained in the cylinder varied considerably from country to country, and most used a light and a heavy canister, the latter for the longer ranges. Iron balls were normally used, as they did not become distorted under the impact of the discharge and the ricochet value was good, but the Austrians used lead balls at least for their light canister. Britain used two weights of ball, $1\frac{1}{4}$oz and $3\frac{1}{4}$oz; Austria normally used 3oz for heavy canister; France used three weights ranging from 2oz to 4oz, the two lighter ones being mixed in the light canister. The number of balls per cylinder varies in the sources consulted and Table E is therefore only representative, to give some indication of the number. Most sources, for example, quote $41 \times 3\frac{1}{4}$oz balls for British 6pdr. heavy canister, which gives a total weight of over eight pounds, whereas the canister would have been made up to the weight of only six pounds, including the cylinder. I have shown $31 \times 3\frac{1}{4}$oz balls, though it could possibly have been 41×2oz balls.

It was common practice to load roundshot and then canister for the same discharge, to deal with mass attacks at close range; the canister cut down the leading ranks while the roundshot tore through the length of the columns, though at point-blank ranges two rounds of canister were frequently loaded instead.

Heavy canister is sometimes referred to as grape, but this was an entirely different form of projectile, consisting of nine balls wired together on a stand and enclosed in a canvas bag. It was used only by the siege trains and naval forces during the Napoleonic Wars.

Common shell was a hollow iron sphere containing a bursting charge of gunpowder, ignited by a fuze which was itself ignited by the flash of the propellant charge. The aim was to explode the sphere in the immediate vicinity of the enemy by means of the fuze, and this called for a large bursting charge and a relatively thin shell (the shell walls were about one-sixth of the shell's diameter) so that the casing broke into numerous fragments, moving forward at high velocity. This made the shell too large and fragile to be fired with a large propellant charge from a gun, and therefore the shell was fired only from howitzers and mortars, being the main projectile of the field howitzer. Theoretically it should have been possible for gunners during the Napoleonic Wars to fire small shells from guns using a reduced charge, but this was not realized at the time.

The fuze was of either reed or drilled beechwood containing strands of quick-match and a composition of saltpetre, sulphur and mealed powder. The top was capped with parchment and the outside marked with cuts spaced at half seconds of burning time apart. The gunner had to cut the fuze to the required setting and insert it into the shell before firing, and to speed up this process it was not uncommon for some fuzes to be cut to the lengths probably required in the forthcoming battle and inserted into shells which were then stacked in their respective batches.

There was one other type of projectile common to all countries, although it was rarely used. This was an incendiary shell known as 'carcass', and

TABLE E: Canister

Country	Piece	No. of balls (light canister)	No. of balls (heavy canister)
Austria	3pdr.	?	30
	6pdr.	60	28
	12pdr.	120	?
	7pdr. how.	–	120
Britain	6pdr.	85	31 (?)
	9pdr.	180	44
	5.5in. how.	–	100
France	4pdr.	63	28
	8pdr.	112	41
	12pdr.	112	46
	6in. how.	–	60

was originally of oblong form, made from canvas reinforced with iron hoops and quilted with cord, and containing a mixture of turpentine, tallow, resin, saltpetre, sulphur and antimony, which was poured into the shell and allowed to harden. A fuze containing powder was ignited by the propellant charge. During the Napoleonic Wars a spherical form was developed, with between two and five vents which were filled with powder to form fuzes. These fuzes ignited the incendiary mixture on discharge and allowed egress for the resulting flames. The spherical carcass was not always successful, as the shell walls had to be thin to allow room for a fair quantity of incendiary, and there were many instances of the shells breaking up in the barrel. For this reason the oblong variety persisted until about the time of Waterloo.

Carcass was almost impossible to extinguish and could burn for from three to twelve minutes, depending on calibre. It was fired only by howitzers and mortars, for the reasons given under common shell.

Unique to Britain was another form of shell,

known at the time as 'spherical case-shot'. This was invented by Lieutenant Shrapnel in 1784, but was not tested in action until April 1804, at Fort Amsterdam, Surinam, against the Dutch. Its first recorded use in the Peninsular War is in 1808 at Rolica. No other European country succeeded in copying it for more than 25 years.

Spherical case could be fired by both guns and howitzers, and combined the advantages of shell and canister to give better results at the longer ranges. It consisted of a hollow iron sphere filled with musket balls (27 to 85 for the 6pdr., 41 to 127 for the 9pdr., 153 for the 5.5in. howitzer) and a bursting charge which was ignited by a fuze. However, unlike that of the shell, the bursting charge only had to be strong enough to break open the casing, as the balls then continued under their own velocity, and this enabled the weight of casing and charge to be reduced.

The British introduced another revolutionary projectile to European warfare—the rocket. War rockets were first encountered by the British army at Seringapatam in 1792, where a good many British soldiers were wounded by them; and soon

British shrapnel with balls and powder mixed; common shell with a charge only; and gauges. (R. Wilkinson-Latham)

French gyn for lifting barrels on and off their carriages. Its use is illustrated in Plate F.

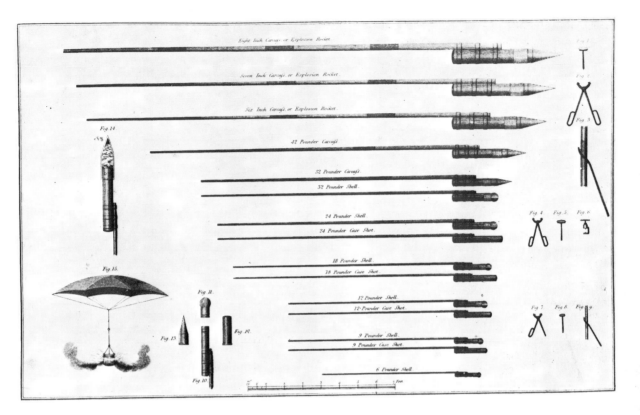

British rocket ammunition and tools. 14 and 15 represent a form of flare: figures 10–13 alternative methods of arranging the different ammunition. (R. Wilkinson-Latham)

afterwards General Desaguliers attempted to make large war rockets at Woolwich, but failed. The work was taken up by Colonel Congreve (son of Sir William), who at that date was in the Hanoverian army but attached to the Royal Laboratory at Woolwich. In 1805 he succeeded in designing the first relatively efficient military rockets in Europe.

These first rockets were made from layers of paper filled with an incendiary composition, and it was intended to use them against Boulogne Harbour in November that year. However, a change of wind prevented them coming into action. In 1806 sheet iron replaced the paper casing, and in October that year Boulogne was badly damaged by 200 rockets fired from eighteen boats in half an hour. The following year 40,000 incendiary rockets practically destroyed Copenhagen. A similar attack at Walcheren was also successful.

In later years a basic hollow iron head was introduced which could be used to make a number of different projectiles, and incendiary rockets were restricted to the siege artillery. These heads were elliptical in shape to reduce air resistance. The lighter rockets used by the field

artillery weighed 6, 9, 12 and 18lbs., and came in three sections: charge, projectile, and a stabilizing stick which was attached by three metal bands round the base of the rocket. The 18pdr. rocket could be armed with either shell or a 9pdr. roundshot; the 12pdr. with a 6pdr. roundshot; the 9pdr. with a grenade; and the 6pdr. with either shell or a 3pdr. roundshot. The 9pdrs., 12pdrs. and 18pdrs. could also be armed with canister by placing musket balls in a chamber at the top of the warhead with a bursting charge behind them.

All exploding rockets had external paper fuzes which were ignited by the propellant flash, the fuze being cut to the required length before loading. This fuze was connected to the bursting charge by quick match held in a tube fixed to the outside of the rocket.

Experiments were also carried out between 1810 and 1820 with infantry rockets, designed to be fired from the shoulder, and a series of these with removable or retractable flashguards may be seen in the Tower of London Armouries. Little is known about their origins, and it is possible they were still at the development stage when the Napoleonic Wars ended.

Austria took the Congreve rocket into service in 1808 and developed a two-barrelled 5cm. rocket launcher which weighed only 19lbs. This could fire a 6pdr. or 12pdr. shell. Heavier rockets were also developed for siege work, but no further details have been discovered by this writer, apart from the fact that all rocketry was handled by a *Feuerwerkscorps*! It is most likely that Austrian rockets were not actually used in action during the Napoleonic Wars.

The proportions of the various projectiles carried by the vehicles of the artillery companies of the various major powers varied according to the calibre and type of piece, and the type of action anticipated. Table F, although incomplete, gives a reasonable idea of the proportions. These proportions and amounts gave an adequate supply of ammunition immediately available to the pieces in their firing positions, but it should be remembered that some pieces had more than one caisson and these other caissons waited some thirty yards to the rear in a safe spot. (For example, the British 6pdr. had a further 220 rounds and the 9pdr. a further 160 rounds available in their first-line ammunition wagons.) Such precautions were necessary not only to prevent the unnecessary loss of men and horses, but more importantly to ensure the artillery was not deprived of ammunition by the destruction of reserve caissons.

The ammunition immediately available was quite capable of keeping the pieces firing continuously for an hour at a standard rate of say one round per minute and, as can be seen from the table, the lighter pieces had the potential to fire continuously for an hour at a much faster rate. It would have been most unusual for such rapid and continuous fire to take place, either in support of attacks or in repulsing enemy attacks; in battle the rate would have averaged much less than one round per minute. The exception would have been counter-battery fire.

Because individual targets such as guns and their crews were far more difficult to hit, it normally took more than an hour of intensive bombardment to neutralize an enemy battery, and consequently counter-battery fire was rare. Companies engaging in counter-battery fire had to watch their supply of ammunition carefully, not only in order to maintain their fire, but also so as not to be caught short of ammunition by a surprise infantry (or more particularly, cavalry) attack. At Waterloo, for example, Wellington forbade counter-battery fire in order to ensure sufficient ammunition was always available to deal with infantry and cavalry attacks.

French gun with horse artillery type of limber, bearing an ammunition chest and seat for gunners. (Musée de l'Armée)

TABLE F: Ammunition Carried

Piece	Position	Ball	Canister (L+H)	Shell	Case	Carcass	Total per gun
British 6pdr. HA	*Gun axle box	8					
	Gun limber	32	5+5				
	Wagon limber	32	4+4				
	Wagon body	60	5+5		20		
	Totals	132	14+14		20		180
British 9pdr.	Gun limber	26	3+3				
	Wagon limber	26	3+3				
	Wagon body	36	2+2		12		
	Totals	88	8+8		12		116
British 5.5in. how.	—		0+8	32	42	2	84
French 4pdr.	Trail chest	18					
	Caisson	100	26+24				
	Totals	118	26+24				168
French 8pdr.	Trail chest	15					
	Caisson	62	20+10				
	Totals	77	20+10				107
French 12pdr.	Trail chest	9					
	Caisson	48	8+12				
	Totals	57	8+12				77
French 6in. how.	Trail chest		0+4**				
	Caisson		0+7	49			
	Totals		0+11	49			60
Prussian 6pdr. HA	Limber	45	15				
	Caisson	90	25				
	Totals	135	40				175
Prussian 6pdr. FA	Limber	45	25				
	Caisson	143	45				
	Totals	188	70				258
Prussian 12pdr.	Limber	12	9				
	Caisson	70	25				
	Totals	82	34				116
Prussian 7pdr. how. HA	Limber		6	14			
	Caisson		16	49	5***		
	Totals		22	63	5		90

Piece	Position	Ball	Canister (L+H)	Shell	Case	Carcass	Total per gun
Prussian							
7pdr. how.	Limber		6	14			
FA	Caisson		20	60		5***	
	Totals		26	74		5	105
Prussian							
7pdr. how.	Limber		6	14			
(how. btrys.)	Caisson		13	40		4***	
****	Totals		19	54		4	77
Prussian							
10pdr. how.	Limber		4	4			
	Caisson		8	36		4***	
	Totals		12	40		4	56
Austria:	(Totals only)						
3pdr.							150 ball
							70 can.
6pdr. FA							160–180 ball
							50 can.
12pdr.							120–160 ball
							30 can.
6pdr. HA							90 ball
							40 can.
7pdr. how.							120–140 shell
							20 can.
Russia:	(Totals only: in each case, 5 rounds from the total quoted were canister, carried on the carriages.)						
6pdr.							77
12pdr.							54
10pdr. how.							54
20pdr. how.							40

Notes

* One contemporary source states that 6 ball and 6 canister were carried in one axle box, and tools, etc., in the other; that there were a further 6 ball and 4 canister without fixed charges in a locker under the gun; and that the limber held 16 ball and 16 canister. Obviously the ratio of ammunition types varied according to the anticipated type of action, but the table gives typical proportions.

** Alternatively listed as 4 shell in the trail chest, and 11 canister and 49 ball in the caisson.

*** Two of which were 'star-shells' in each case.

**** No limber ammunition before January 1813.

A brief résumé of the ammunition carried by the French and British pieces will show that there was little danger of running out of ammunition even during a major battle:

French 12pdr. with 5 caissons, 349 rounds per piece.
,, 8pdr. ,, 3 ,, 291 ,, ,, ,,
,, 4pdr. ,, 2 ,, 318 ,, ,, ,,
,, 6in. howitzer with 3 caissons, 172 rounds per piece

British light 6pdr., 180 plus 220 in 1st line wagons = 276 per piece
,, 9pdr., 116 plus 160 in 1st line wagons = 400 per piece

At Waterloo 78 British guns and howitzers fired some 10,000 rounds, an average of 129 rounds per piece. The highest single expenditure was Sandham's Company: 1,100 rounds at 183 rounds per piece, well within the totals readily available.

However, loss of ammunition due to destruction of caissons could cause the artillery to run out of ammunition, though such instances were rare.

In 1813–14 the French did in fact experience difficulties over ammunition supply, even though in the earlier years their supply system had been superior to that of the Allies, with a unified system under the Artillery Train, which handled the whole business from the front line right back to the depots. These later difficulties were not due entirely to shortages or failures by the Train, caused by the tide of the war turning against France, but more to the rapid growth of the artillery arm as the quality of the infantry declined. Thus at Wagram the French fired 96,000 rounds, and at Borodino 91,000, without experiencing any difficulties in supply; but by 1813 their artillery was in severe danger of running out of ammunition on the field of battle. At Leipzig Napoleon's 900 guns and howitzers fired over 200,000 rounds, an average of 222 rounds per piece and therefore still within the number of rounds theoretically available to each piece, but on 18 October only 20,000 rounds remained available for the entire army, and Napoleon

French 6pdr. and carriage of the Gribeauval system, shown here limbered to the old-fashioned type of heavy limber with ammunition chest. In the background is an ammunition caisson with spare wheel, tool-box and standard limber. (Musée de l'Armée)

estimated that he needed at least 30,000. In early 1814 he estimated he would need 400,000 rounds for the forthcoming campaigns, yet the available stock was only 100,000: in this year the French artillery was actually silenced by its lack of ammunition.

The Method of Firing

Artillery pieces could be brought into position, unlimbered, the limber team driven off, and the trail chest unloaded and opened all in one minute. The NCO in charge of each piece would give the order to load and a precise drill would then be carried out, not only to achieve correct and swift firing, but also to ensure no accidents occurred in the heat of battle. A piece could be limbered up again and ready to move in two or three minutes.

In the British artillery there were five gunners directly involved in the loading and firing drill of all pieces. The NCO was known as No. 1, responsible for issuing orders, aiming the piece and observing the fall of shot. He stood at the end of the trail. Two gunners stood in front of the piece, No. 2 the spongeman to the right of the barrel, No. 3 the loader to the left. The other two gunners stood behind the piece, No. 4 the ventsman to the right of the trail, No. 5 the firer to the left. Four

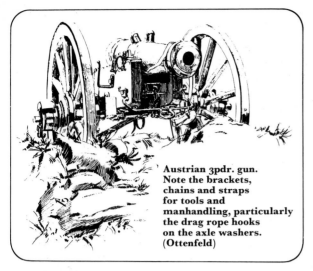

Austrian 3pdr. gun.
Note the brackets,
chains and straps
for tools and
manhandling, particularly
the drag rope hooks
on the axle washers.
(Ottenfeld)

other gunners were responsible for keeping the loader supplied with ammunition.

In the French artillery the number of gunners varied according to the calibre of the piece and they were assisted by infantrymen attached to the crew to keep the loader supplied and to manhandle the piece. The 12pdr. had eight gunners and seven infantrymen, the 8pdr. eight and five, the 4pdr. six and four respectively.

In the Austrian artillery there were six gunners for each piece, assisted by men from *Handlanger* battalions who were not trained gunners but in emergency often acted as such. The 3pdr. had six *Handlanger*, 6pdr. and 7pdr. howitzer had

eight, and the 12pdr. twelve.

Pieces in the Russian light batteries had ten crew members plus another five with the caissons; position batteries had twelve crew plus seven with the caissons.

The numbering of these crews varied, but the drill was more or less the same in each of the artillery corps. Assuming a piece to have been fired, the drill would have been as follows. Because at this date there was no recoil mechanism, the piece had first to be run back to its firing position. Recoil was from four to six feet and the entire crew was needed to run the piece back, using handspikes and drag ropes.

The spongeman then dipped his sponge into a bucket of water and thrust it down the bore to extinguish any smouldering fragments remaining from the previous charge. The loader then placed a new round in the bore, the spongeman reversing his staff to use the rammer at the opposite end to ram the round home. As he did so, the ventsman placed his thumb, protected by a leather thumbstall, over the vent to prevent a rush of air, which might cause a premature explosion if any burning fragments had survived in the bore. Once the round was fully home the ventsman thrust a pricker down the vent to clear it and pierce the cartridge, inserted a firing tube, and checked the elevation for range. While this was being carried out, the No. 1 would be traversing by means

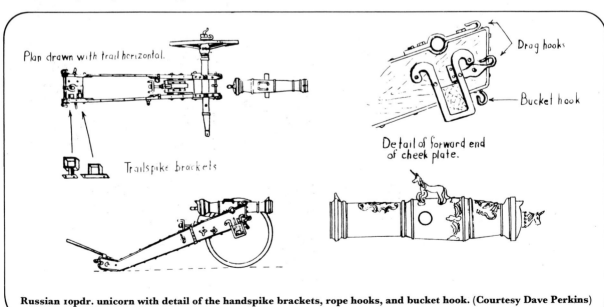

Russian 10pdr. unicorn with detail of the handspike brackets, rope hooks, and bucket hook. (Courtesy Dave Perkins)

Russian gunner with, to scale, examples of
contemporary ammunition types and gauges.
See text for explanatory key.

A

1. Loading a Russian 12pdr. gun

2. Priming a Prussian 6pdr. gun

B

1. Aiming an Austrian 3pdr. gun

2. Running back a French 12pdr. gun

C

1. Harness for Russian team hauling 12pdr. gun

2. (Above) Harness for French team hauling 12pdr. gun
3. (Below) Harness for British team hauling 9pdr. gun

French pontoon wagon; and French pontoon bridge under construction

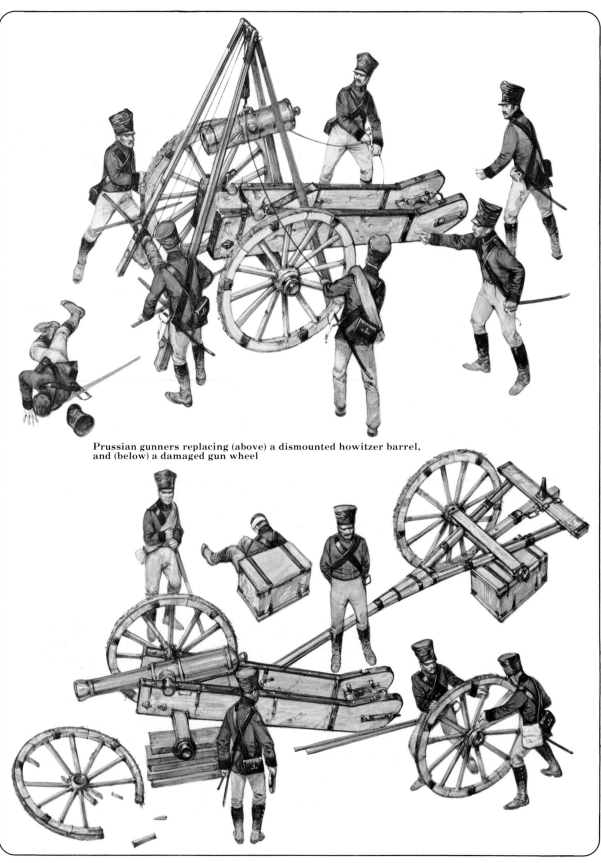

Prussian gunners replacing (above) a dismounted howitzer barrel, and (below) a damaged gun wheel

1. British 12pdr. rocket carriage

2. (Above) 12pdr. rockets ready for ground firing
(Below) 12pdr. rockets ready for high-angle firing

Austrian gunner with, to scale, examples of contemporary tools and accessories. See text for explanatory key.

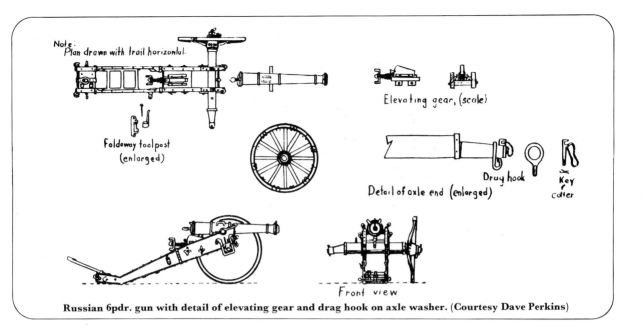

Russian 6pdr. gun with detail of elevating gear and drag hook on axle washer. (Courtesy Dave Perkins)

of a lever or levers in the trail, to aim the piece at its target, a task requiring two men before the lighter trails were introduced. Finally the firer applied his portfire to the firing tube, the piece discharged its projectile, and the whole process started again.

Fixed ammunition and this drill prevented the weather from affecting the charges, and a new firing tube could soon be used if a misfire occurred, but the problem of misfires remained because of overheating during prolonged rapid fire. Under these conditions the vent could become so hot that it was impossible to insert a firing tube without it exploding prematurely, and the ventsman might also be unable to block the vent during loading, even with the protection of his thumbstall. The only solution might be a bucket of water, which was rarely practical in the heat of battle as the only water ready to hand was needed for sponging; it was more common simply to cease firing, or slow the rate of fire. This was the main reason why guns were not deployed individually, as a battery commander could always ensure that one or two pieces were ready for emergencies.

The sponge-rammer consisted of a long staff with at one end a wooden cylinder about a foot long and of the same diameter as the projectile. This was covered with sheepskin or sometimes bristle. At the opposite end was a similar cylinder

of bare wood with the end dished to receive the projectile. Some rammers had the staff marked to indicate when a round was in the bore: this helped prevent double-loading in the confusion of battle. The bucket for the sponge was carried on a hook under the axle-tree. The spongeman might also have a 'wormer', a staff with at one end a device resembling a pair of intertwined corkscrews. This was thrust into the bore and twisted to extract wads of unburnt paper when paper cartridges were still in use. Occasionally the worm might be incorporated in the head of a sponge, enabling both jobs to be done at once.

The handspikes used to move the piece were specially shaped poles up to six feet long, made from ash and sometimes shod with iron. They were strapped to the trail when the piece was limbered up. Two breast chains about three feet long were permanently fastened to the front face of the axle-tree, their free ends hooked up to a fitting in the centre. In action drag ropes were attached to these, and to lugs on the wheel washers, for running the piece back into its firing position.

The vent pricker or priming wire was a sharp-pointed rod, sometimes with a wooden handle, sometimes with the top end just bent over to form a ring. It was used to clear the vent as well as to pierce the charge bag. The vent itself was inclined forward at an angle of 101° (so that the

25

Close-up of the elevating screw mechanism on a British artillery piece.

empty tube was thrown clear of the crew on firing) and consisted of a bush with a hole through it which was only .2 of an inch. Despite the smallness of this hole, gas escaped through it at each firing and gradually burnt away the bushing, until the vent was so large that the piece was unserviceable. Such pieces had then to be sent to the nearest arsenal for the tedious job of re-venting.

In theory pieces could be put out of action, at least temporarily, by driving a long spike of soft iron into the vent. In fact this was rarely done in the field, and no spikes were issued to assault troops or even to gunners.

The firing tubes were made from quills or of tin or copper, and were filled with mealed powder moistened with spirits of wine. These tubes came in different lengths for the various calibres, it not being realized until 1820 that this was not necessary. The bottom end of the tube was cut slantwise, and metal ones were often strengthened with solder, to assist in piercing the cartridge. The top was capped with flannel steeped in a mixture of saltpetre and spirits of wine so that the cap did not have to be removed for firing.

The firing tube was lit by a quick-match held in a wooden handle known as a portfire. Quick-match burnt at about an inch a minute, producing

a fierce heat for improved ignition, and unless engaged in rapid firing it was lit for each discharge and extinguished afterwards. It was relit from the old-fashioned linstock, which held a slow-match, burning at the rate of about four inches per hour, and which was stuck into the ground between every pair of guns.

All fire was by direct line of sight, with the naked eye aligning on the target merely by looking along the barrel, i.e. the top of the base ring to the top of the muzzle. It was common practice, even in the mid-19th century, to find this centre line by placing a spirit-level first on the base ring, then on the muzzle. When the instrument was level on both these places, a plumb bob should show the centre line of the bore, but in practice pieces were still crudely made and such a line on the exterior was unlikely to coincide exactly with the centre line of the bore, particularly in howitzers. Nevertheless, it provided a rough guide, and with notches filed in muzzle and base ring, experienced gunners obtained considerable accuracy by allowing for the known error of their guns. Foresights were eventually cast on the muzzles of some guns, as were fixed rear sights later on.

Correct ranging was also achieved mainly by eye and experience, but was assisted by the elevating screw, which seems to have been in general use by the time of the Napoleonic Wars. It comprised a screw-threaded rod working in a capstan-headed nut secured to the carriage transom or bed. On British pieces the upper end of the rod was either bolted to an eye cast in the cascable or ended in a flat plate on which the breech rested. On the French guns it passed at an angle through the bed transom and raised the whole bed at one end, the other end being hinged to the breast transom. On the 6in. howitzer carriage a rather more complicated system was used, with the screw fitted horizontally through the bed transom and engaging a gear to raise a panel set into the bed. The elevating screw enabled much finer calibration to be achieved, but artillery still relied mainly on the experience of the gunners for accuracy.

Performance

The effectiveness of artillery depends on the calibre and type of piece, the ammunition and charge used, and the elevation and range, but there is another unseen factor that needs to be considered. The artillery of the Napoleonic Wars was not nearly so effective—in terms of casualties—as is often supposed, and at the longer ranges could do little damage, yet it had considerable psychological effect on a battle. The troops were drawn up in column and line, able to see the projectiles wobbling towards them, unable to avoid them or return fire, deafened by the thunderous roar, and shaken by the appalling mess the projectiles made of the men they did hit. Small wonder morale could be so shaken by an artillery bombardment that troops would sometimes break before an attack arrived to their immediate front. The damage done by a 12pdr. ball (4.75in. diameter) and that caused by a 9pdr. ball (4.25in.) was little different, and the additional range of the 12pdr. was seldom used; but the larger pieces produced a more deafening noise on firing, and the whistle of their shot was louder and more eerie. They were comforting things to have in support, unnerving weapons to face; and at Waterloo even the British veterans, who had not encountered 12pdrs. in the field in the Peninsula, were daunted by Napoleon's beloved *belles filles*.

Of all projectiles, roundshot was the most effective and reliable, and it formed about 70 per cent of the ammunition fired. A single roundshot could shatter a wagon or gun carriage, or slice a man or horse in half, and it did this in a noisy and frightening way. At the longer ranges, and if fired at right angles to the target, it had little effect on regiments deployed in line, but it could be devastating when fired enfilade or into a column, ploughing through the ranks with frightful effect. At Waterloo an officer and 25 men of the 40th Foot were killed or wounded by a single shot, though this was the most destructive shot known to the officer who recorded the incident. At effective range perhaps seven or eight killed and wounded might be a more normal result. Regiments, even in line, were sometimes cut to pieces by concentrated artillery fire, yet despite this commanders habitually deployed their troops in the open: Wellington was an exception.

Tests carried out in England in about 1835, using British artillery pieces of the Napoleonic Wars, showed that at a range of 600 yards there was an average error in the horizontal plane of only about 15 feet to left or right of the target. When one considers that the targets often had a wide frontage, it can be seen that at least at this range there were few misses due to error in the horizontal plane. Table G, showing average figures based on tests conducted in England in the 18th and 19th centuries, confirms this:

TABLE G: Percentage of hits

Piece	Range in yards	Percentage of hits
6pdr.	520	82
	950	40
	1,200	17
12pdr.	600	87
	950	40
	1,300	17

The hits listed in the table were recorded against a line. When considering casualties inflicted one should remember the shot might continue on its way to hit a second or even third line beyond, and in the case of a column the percentage of casualties would have been considerably higher. Austrian tests indicated that at 800 yards guns could expect between 40–70 per cent hits against a company-sized target in line, but that this fell markedly to only 15 per cent at 1,200 yards.

The way in which the range of a piece is affected by the calibre, charge and elevation is illustrated by Table H. The pieces used by the other countries are so similar, and their results so little different, that it is not worth quoting them separately here. However, most countries used the howitzer at 30° elevation, whereas the maximum elevation used by the British was normally 12° and by the Russian 'unicorns' 20°. This suggests the Russians and British regarded the howitzer as more of a gun than a mortar, while the reverse was true in other countries (Table I).

Roundshot was normally fired at a flat trajectory in order to obtain the greatest possible impact and the maximum zone of effect. The roundshot would hit the ground at a comparatively short distance from the piece, a point known as first graze, then ricochet to a point up to half as far again, known as the second graze, where some 80 per cent would ricochet again. Thus at zero elevation a French 8pdr. or British 9pdr. ball might be expected to hit the ground at about 400 yards, ricochet to 600, and ricochet again up to about 700 yards. It might then bounce again or roll another 50 yards or so before coming to a stop. During all this time the ball was travelling at below the height of a man and would destroy, kill or maim anything in its path. A 4pdr. to 6pdr. ball would first graze at *circa* 300 yards and continue to around 550 yards: a 12pdr. ball would first graze at 600 yards and continue to about 1,100 yards. The state of the ground naturally affected the ricochet.

To obtain greater ranges the piece had to be elevated, and this not only decreased the amount of ricochet but could also mean the ball would travel part of its distance above a man's height. At one-quarter degree elevation the point of first graze from an 8pdr. or 9pdr. ball would be increased from 400 yards to 500-600, the ball travelling perhaps 1,000 yards in all, all at below a man's height. At one degree of elevation the ball would rise above a man's height, have a first graze point of about 700 yards, and ricochet to 1,000 yards. The angle would probably prevent a second ricochet and therefore only the last

TABLE H: Approximate Range Limits (yards)

Country	Piece	Max. range	Effective range	Canister
Austria	3pdr.	900	350-450	300
	6pdr.	1,000	400-500	400
	12pdr.	1,200	700	500
	7pdr. how.	1,350	700	500
Britain	6pdr.	1,200-1,500	600-700	350-400
	9pdr.	1,700	800-900	450
	5.5in. how.	1,700	700	500
France	4pdr.	1,200	700	400
	6pdr.	1,500	800	400-450
	8pdr.	1,500	800	500-550
	12pdr.	1,800	900	600
	6in. how.	1,200	700	500-600
Prussia	3pdr.	1,000	450	300
	6pdr.	1,500	500-600	400
	12pdr.	2,000	900	550
	7pdr. how.	1,600	700	550
	10pdr. how.	1,950	700	550
Russia	6pdr.	1,500	800	400
	12pdr.	2,000	700-900	500-600
	'Unicorns'	1,750-2,500	700	500-600

The Russian 20pdr. unicorn had a range of 2,000 yards at 7° and 1,100 yards at 5°, these two angles marking the normal maximum and effective ranges respectively. Ranges below 700 yards were outside the limit of the fuze.

TABLE I: British Howitzer Ranges

Piece	Shell Weight	Charge Weight	Ranges at degrees of elevation:							
			12°	10°	5°	4°	3°	2°	1°	0°
Light 5.5in.	16lbs	1lb	1,400	1,200	850	750	600	450	250	150
Heavy 5.5in.	16lbs	2lbs	1,700	1,500	975	850	700	550	400	250

TABLE J: British Cannon Ranges

Elevation	Range, light 6pdr. with 1½lb charge	Range, heavy 6pdr. and 9pdr. with 3lbs charge
Roundshot:		
0°	200 yards	300
1°	600	700
2°	800	1,000
3°	1,000	1,200
4°	1,200	1,400

Spherical case:	Spread of bullets between:
1¾°	640 & 920 yards
2¼°	930 & 1,180
3¼°	1,160 & 1,390
4⅜°	1,360 & 1,570

300 yards would have been below a man's height. At two degrees of elevation the point of first graze would be about 900 yards, but the angle would be so great that the ball would hardly bounce at all.

From this it can be seen that guns were rarely elevated beyond one degree, as even at this angle some 700 yards in front of the gun were safe from the shot. There was no point, however, in loss of impact by ricocheting to your target, and it was normal to aim for first graze just short of the target and rely on the long zone of effectiveness thereafter to achieve the maximum effect.

It can be seen from this that it was not normally possible (or advisable) to fire over the heads of friendly troops, unless on *markedly* higher ground. In fact firing over your own troops was discouraged under any conditions, as it inevitably meant a shortening of the lethal zone and could even cause the shot to bury itself harmlessly if the earth were soft. This was also true of plunging fire from high ground.

Earthworks were proof against 6pdr. ball and below at the longer ranges. At Chiclana in 1811 a French redoubt received 93 hits in fifteen minutes without sustaining a single casualty; but the Austrians estimated that at about 600–650 yards their 3pdr. could penetrate five feet of rammed earth, their 6pdr. seven feet, and 12pdr. seven and a half feet.

Common shell should not be associated with modern H.E. shells: it was comparatively feeble and inaccurate, being effective only at ranges of between 700 and 1,200 yards, and against stationary targets. This was because reliable fuzes were hard to come by and it required a very experienced gunner to cut a fuze correctly in the heat of battle. Fuzes frequently went out, or were cut too short and exploded the shell in the air, or cut too long and left the shell smouldering on the ground, where it might be extinguished by a brave man. They were also subject to the state of the ground: Waterloo, for example, was a bad day for shell because the ground was so soft that they buried themselves in the mud, where their explosions were rendered harmless. The normal effective burst radius of a shell was about 25 yards.

The limit of 700 yards in range was also caused by the fuze, which had to have a certain proportion inside the casing. Therefore, even though the fuze outside the shell was cut short, sufficient fuze remained for the burning time equal to a minimum of 700 yards: to cut the fuze shorter would have left nothing outside the shell to be ignited by the flash of the discharge.

Spherical case shot had a similar burst radius to shell, and range limits of 700–1,500 yards. It was remarkably reliable for its time but not nearly so effective as is often suggested. Certainly it was useful for counter-battery fire and was hated by the French gunners, who had no reply to it. Wellington wrote to Shrapnel after the Vimeiro campaign: 'The spherical case shot had the best effect in producing the defeat of the enemy.' He revised this opinion on seeing a captured French general, wounded by case shot, who suffered no permanent injury although his face and head were peppered with the balls. Wellington had the casings filled with musket balls and these were more effective: at the crossing of the Douro in 1813 a single round dropped every man and horse serving the first French gun to come into action.

Nevertheless, technical difficulties prevented the projectile being fully effective at the time. Tests carried out in 1812 showed that only 2 to 17 per cent of the bullets were hitting target screens at ranges of 700–1,500 yards. Tests by the

TABLE K: Spherical Case

Piece	Elevation	Charge	Fuze	Range
9pdr.	$1\frac{1}{4}°$	3lbs	.225in.	650 yds
	$1\frac{3}{4}°$	,,	.4in.	900
	$2\frac{1}{2}°$	,,	.6in.	1,100
heavy	$1\frac{1}{2}°$	2lbs	.225in.	650
6pdr.	$1\frac{3}{4}°$	,,	.45in.	900
	$2\frac{3}{4}°$	,,	.65in.	1,100
light	$1\frac{1}{2}°$	$1\frac{1}{2}$lb	.3in.	650
6pdr.	$2°$	,,	.5in.	900
	$2\frac{3}{4}°$	,,	.65in.	1,100
heavy	$3\frac{1}{4}°$	2lbs	.45in.	650
5.5in.	$4\frac{3}{4}°$	,,	.65in.	900
how.	$6\frac{1}{4}°$	,,	.65in.	1,100
light	$5\frac{3}{4}°$	1lb	.6in.	650
5.5in.	$8°$	,,	.9in.	900
how.	$10°$	,,	1.33in.	1,100

Madras artillery gave an average of 10 per cent. The unreliability of the projectiles was tested in 1819 and 1852, giving failure rates of 17 per cent and 22 per cent respectively, mostly due to premature explosion. It was thought that such failures were due to faulty fuze setting; but the tests of 1852–54 proved that they were caused by friction between powder and balls during firing and flight, and at this later date the two were separated by a diaphragm.

Both shell and shrapnel were used most effectively at long range, where they could achieve better results than plunging fire with roundshot. They were also more effective than roundshot on broken ground, for obvious reasons. They could also be fired over the heads of friendly troops to reach an enemy behind obstacles or on reverse slopes: Frederick the Great used howitzers for this purpose during the Seven Years War. This valuable asset was ignored during the Napoleonic Wars by all except the Prussian artillery, which in August 1813 received the following instruction: 'Should the enemy be on the reverse side of a slope, it will be advantageous to concentrate the howitzers, as a large number of shells thrown on one spot will produce a fearful effect.' Think how such use by the French might have affected the British position at Waterloo.

Canister was used at the closer ranges and was usually very effective, despite the fact that much of the cone-shaped burst went into the ground or over the men's heads, while up to 50 per cent of the remaining balls might pass through the gaps between the men. Records of British tests reveal that 41 per cent of 6pdr. canister balls obtained hits at 400 yards, 23 per cent at 600 yards. (For a battery this was equivalent to a 500-man battalion delivering a volley at 100 yards.) The Madras artillery tests, of over 1,000 firings, show the following results with the same calibre piece: 55 hits at 200 yards; 36 hits at 400 yards; six hits at 600 yards.

Canister was not infallible, even at close ranges, and there are many recorded instances of misses, perhaps because in the stress of the moment the elevation of the piece was incorrect, as Captain Mercer reports at Waterloo: 'The French artillerymen . . . opened a fire of case-shot on us, but without effect, for we retreated to our ridge, without the loss of a man or even any wounded, though the range could not have been above 200 yards.'

Heavy canister was used at the longer ranges, and the French seem to have employed this over much greater distances than other countries. British artillery, for example, did not normally fire canister at ranges exceeding 350 yards, though the tests show it could still have a good effect at 400 yards: this was probably due to the relatively small number of canister rounds carried. Probably because of using artillery boldly in support of attacks, the French on the other hand fired heavy canister at ranges of 500–600 yards, and one French author claims that it was fired from 12pdrs. at 800 yards.

The rocket had a reputation for being highly erratic on land, which is not surprising considering many were discharged without the benefit of a launcher: at sea, fired from correct launchers, they proved effective. However, this was against very large targets, and in Wellington's own words: 'I do not want to set fire to any town, and I do not know of any other use for rockets.' Nevertheless, a rocket detachment did good service during the crossing of the Adour, before the battle of Orthes, destroying three French gun boats and forcing a sloop to retire, then being amongst the first troops across the river and putting a French column to flight. Another detachment was used successfully at Leipzig where, according to one eye witness, a whole brigade surrendered after receiving fire for a few minutes.

Rate of fire was estimated at ten per minute, as the rocket had only to be placed in position and the fuze lit, so an intense barrage could be discharged. Effective ranges when fired from the ground were 800–1,000 yards for the smallest rockets, 1,000–1,200 for the larger, though maximum ranges were 2,000 yards for the 6pdr., 3,000 for the 9pdr. and 12pdr.

The accuracy of roundshot, shell, spherical case and canister, and also perhaps their range, was also affected by 'windage', the difference between the calibre of the piece and the diameter of its projectile; the difference being necessary for loading and to prevent pieces exploding through projectiles jamming in the bore. Windage was partly overcome by the wooden sabot, which was mostly burnt away by the time the projectile left the barrel. The French seem to have worked with a much smaller windage than other countries and this may have been the factor which enabled them to engage at rather longer ranges than their opponents.

From the above it can be seen that the various projectiles had definite advantages and restrictions which governed their use: shell (and spherical case for the British) was used at extreme ranges and down to 700 yards: roundshot from about 1,000 to 500 yards: heavy canister perhaps on average from 500 to 250 yards (from 350 for the British): and light canister from 250 yards to zero. The British 'Artillery Officers' Training Manual' gives the following table of ammunition types used against attacks:

Cavalry attack

1,500–650 yards	7 spherical case and shell	
650–350 yards	2 roundshot	
350– 0 yards	2 case shot	*Total* 11 rounds

Infantry attack

1,500–650 yards	19 spherical case and shell	
650–350 yards	7 roundshot	
350– 0 yards	2 case	*Total* 28 rounds

Other countries would have used common shell instead of spherical case.

The German historian Müller, who served in the King's German Legion, assessed the rate of casualties that might be inflicted by 6pdrs. during such attacks as follows (though he allowed a more rapid rate of fire than that given above):

Cavalry

1,600–800 yards	4 killed	2 wounded
800–400 yards	6 killed	4 wounded
400– 0 yards	9 killed	23 wounded

Infantry

1,600–1,200 yards	4 killed	4 wounded
1,200– 800 yards	8 killed	2 wounded
800– 400 yards	16 killed	10 wounded
400– 0 yards	30 killed	90 wounded

These figures also provide an approximate rate of fire. At drill light guns are recorded as achieving eight rounds per minute and heavy guns five rounds per minute, but this was under perfect conditions. In action it took much longer to run up a gun after recoil and re-lay it on the target; and the supply of ammunition, exhaustion of the crew, casualties, and the obscuring of targets by friendly forces and smoke, would all combine to reduce the possible rate of fire. The maximum rate, laid down in the manuals and well authenticated by records, seems to have been two roundshot or three canister per minute for guns, with perhaps three rounds in two minutes for howitzers. The heavier pieces, like the 12pdrs., were naturally slower, at one roundshot per minute. There can be little doubt that in battle gunners often could not see their targets, either because of the smoke from their own guns or those of the enemy, and it is quite likely that firing came in short, concentrated bursts, with one round per minute a normal *average* rate of fire.

★　　★　　★

Field artillery was quite capable of keeping up with the rest of the army, provided the weather was not wet. Ten to fifteen miles a day was an average march, but between 40 and 50 miles could be covered in 24 hours in emergencies. Rivers up to a depth of four feet could be forded without trouble, and deeper rivers were crossed by rafts. A variety of tools was carried, and the considerable manpower available from the crews meant that artillery could undertake almost any task, from clearing a way through hedges and woods to improving cart tracks or putting their shoulders behind the wheels to help the draught teams.

Organization

Austria

During the peace of 1806–09 the Austrian army was completely reorganized and the artillery was concentrated as an independent supporting arm after the French style, with the pieces organized into Brigade and Position Batteries. The Brigade Batteries consisted of eight 3pdrs. or 6pdrs. with their caissons and three baggage wagons, and were attached to the infantry brigades for close support. The Position Batteries consisted of either four 6pdrs. and two 7pdr. howitzers, or four 12pdrs. and two 7pdr. howitzers, or four 18pdrs. and two 10pdr. howitzers. These were allocated to division, corps and army reserves respectively. Each had its caissons plus four baggage wagons.

The Cavalry Batteries could not be called horse artillery in the strict sense as, although there were spare horses, not all the personnel was individually mounted, most riding on the 'Wurst' caissons and padded seat of the gun trail. These batteries had five 6pdrs. and one 7pdr. howitzer with their accompanying caissons, plus three baggage

wagons and 24 munition pack-horses with twelve mounted pack drivers.

Manning these batteries were four regiments of artillery, each of sixteen companies of *kanoniers*: a company usually manned four batteries. Each company had at full establishment 187 personnel. The regiment's size was increased by several companies of *Handlanger*, a company of *bombardiers* to man the howitzers, and in a few cases a *Feuerwerkscompagnie*.

The Transport (*Fuhrwesen*) Corps provided teams and drivers for these batteries. The corps was divided into *Fuhrwesencorps Artillerie-Bespanungdivision*, each of 73 personnel and 180 horses, sufficient to move three batteries. The *Fuhrwesencorps* allocated to the horse artillery had 200 men and 200 horses to move two batteries.

The ratio of artillery pieces to men was, at its peak, 3.5 to every one thousand men.

Britain

In 1803 the Royal Artillery consisted of eight battalions, each of ten companies: a 9th Battalion was raised in 1806 and a 10th in 1808. When necessary these companies were allocated guns, draught teams and drivers, the whole unit then being known as an artillery brigade, the modern 'battery'. The authorized establishment of a company was 145 personnel, but field strength was usually between 110–130.

Each of the foot artillery brigades had six pieces, usually five guns and one howitzer, although all-gun brigades were not uncommon and there were occasionally all-howitzer batteries. At this date the standard pieces were the 6pdr. gun and 5.5in. howitzer: the 9pdr. gun was not reintroduced until 1808.

In addition to their pieces and limbers each brigade also required eight ammunition wagons, three baggage wagons, a field forge and spare wheel wagon, together with some 200 horses and mules to pull them, and about 100 drivers. Drivers and teams were provided by the Corps of Artillery Drivers.

The Royal Horse Artillery, in which most gunners were mounted on horses (some rode the vehicles), consisted in 1801 of seven troops, increased to twelve by 1806. Equipment in 1809 was normally five 6pdrs. and one 5.5in. howitzer,

British 9pdr. brass gun on Congreve block trail carriage. Note axle boxes. (National Army Museum)

with their limbers, six ammunition wagons, three baggage wagons, a spare wheel wagon and mobile forge. (At Waterloo an RHA 9pdr. troop had nine ammunition wagons and one each spare wheel carriage, forge, and baggage wagons, and a two-wheeled cart.) At full strength there were 106 personnel, including 80 gunners, with 106 horses. To these totals were added approximately 120 draught animals and 60 drivers. The latter, although originally supplied by the Corps of Artillery Drivers, were incorporated into each troop as an integral part of the unit.

The 1st and 2nd Rocket Troops, officially added to the artillery establishment in January 1813, were classed as RHA because of their mobility. The recommended organization in 1814 was 178 personnel, three heavy and three light limbers, six ammunition carts, one forge cart and 164 horses. The 6pdr. rockets were carried in pairs in saddle holsters and bundles of sticks were supported in a small bucket forward of the offside stirrup. Every third mounted gunner carried a small trough on his saddlebag to discharge these rockets along the ground.

A single mountain battery was formed for the crossing of the Pyrenees into France. This was equipped with six 3pdrs., the barrel carried by one mule, the carriage being dismantled and carried by two other mules. The personnel were a mixture of British and Portuguese. The battery was disbanded at the end of the campaign.

The King's German Legion had two horse artillery troops and three foot artillery brigades by early 1805. The troops each had five 6pdrs. and one 5.5in. howitzer: two of the brigades had four 6pdrs. and two 5.5in. howitzers, the other had four 9pdrs. and two howitzers. Other organization was approximately the same as the British.

France

From 1803 there were successive increases in the establishment of the artillery, and separate Guard units were organized. Some detail of these changes, establishment and equipment is set out below.

Horse Artillery of the Guard A light artillery company had been formed for the Consular Guard in 1799: it was expanded to a regiment of six companies in three squadrons in 1806. In 1808 it was reduced to two squadrons of two companies each, and remained at this strength until 1815. Each company had 97 personnel and was equipped with six 6pdrs., usually captured pieces, or four 6pdrs. and two 6in. howitzers. In late 1813 a Young Guard company was formed but was disbanded in 1814.

Foot Artillery of the Guard Created in April 1808 at a strength of six còmpanies, each of 84 men. Three companies of Young Guard were added in June 1809, and in 1813 this was increased to 16 companies. In 1815 there were only the six companies of the Old Guard, the Young Guard companies having been reduced to Line in 1814. The Old Guard companies were equipped with 12pdrs. from the start, though the number appears to have varied from only four per company in 1809 to eight per company by 1812. Sometimes these later companies had six guns and two 24pdr. howitzers. The Young Guard companies had eight 4pdrs. each, for supporting infantry attacks.

Line Horse Artillery There were six regiments in 1804, increased to seven in 1810, though this 7th Regiment was soon absorbed into the 1st and 4th. Each regiment had six companies (from 1805 there was also a depot company). In 1813 the 1st to 3rd Regiments had a seventh company. Each company had about 79 personnel and was normally equipped with four 6pdrs. and two 6in. howitzers, though sometimes 4pdr. guns were used.

Line Foot Artillery There were eight regiments in 1804, rising to nine in 1810. Each regiment had 22 companies in 1804, increased to 28 companies in 1813. Equipment was six 8pdrs. and two 6in. howitzers, though all-gun companies were common.

Napoleon was of the opinion that a single gun, the 6pdr., could beneficially replace the 4pdr. and 8pdr., provided the reserve artillery had 12pdrs., and that the 6in. howitzer should be replaced by a 24pdr. one (75 rounds of 24pdr. ammunition could be carried in a caisson compared to 50 of the 6in.). Accordingly a programme was begun to equip the Foot Artillery with 6pdrs. (and 24pdr. howitzers), enabling the French to profitably employ the mass of captured ammunition of this calibre. Unfortunately for the French, the outbreak of war in 1805 caused the new 6pdr. to be rushed into production without trials and this soon led to adverse comments from the gunners on its performance. The French 6pdr. was eventually abandoned, although the captured pieces continued to serve: in 1807 Soult's corps had 48 pieces, of which 42 were of Austrian origin. By 1812 many of the 4pdrs. and 8pdrs. had in fact been replaced by 6pdrs. and 12pdrs., and the 6in. howitzer by the 24pdr. one; but over 1,200 pieces were lost in Russia, and

French 12pdr. and carriage of the Gribeauval system. (National Army Museum)

further losses in 1813 meant that the original pieces had to be reissued to keep the artillery up to strength. There can be little doubt that the decision to change pieces in 1803, and the renewal of hostilities in 1805, contributed greatly to the deficiencies in the artillery arm in the 1813 and 1814 campaigns.

Each infantry division was allocated one foot and one horse company, and each light cavalry division had one horse company. As early as 1804–05 an artillery reserve was in the process of being formed, comprising about 25 percent of the pieces available. The increase in the number of 12pdrs. meant that more companies could be equipped with six 12pdrs. and two 6in. howitzers, although the majority retained the 8pdrs.; and there were usually two 12pdr. companies allocated to each Corps reserve. The formation of the Foot Artillery of the Guard in 1808 switched all 12pdrs. to the Guard, and the Guard Artillery became in effect the reserve artillery of the army.

Because of the mass of captured Austrian and Prussian *matériel* in June 1809 Napoleon reintroduced battalion guns for the 63 regiments in Austria. The 1st Battalion of each regiment received two 3pdrs. or two 4pdrs., three ammunition caissons, and eleven other vehicles. These were manned by men from the battalion, a squad of 20 gunners and two artisans, and two squads each of 20 drivers. This organization was theoretically dissolved by a decree issued in April 1810, but re-established for the 16 regiments of the Corps of Observation of the Elbe in February 1811. These 16 regiments each received four 3pdrs. or 4pdrs., six caissons and eleven other vehicles. The gunnery squad now had 36 gunners and four artisans; a second squad of 24 drivers and 48 horses hauled the guns and caissons; and a third squad of 28 men and 52 horses took care of the other vehicles.

Most regiments appear to have had two guns for the 1812 campaign. Not one of these guns was saved during the retreat from Moscow, and that was the end of regimental artillery in Napoleon's armies.

In 1804 the Line Artillery Train had ten companies, each of 76 men. This rose to eleven companies in 1805, 13 in 1808, and 14 in 1810. The strength of these companies could be doubled in times of war by raising auxiliary companies, but these were always short of vehicles.

A battalion of six companies of Artillery Train of the Guard had been formed during the Consulate period. By 1807 there were two battalions, each of twelve companies, and by February 1813 there were three battalions. In April that year a second regiment was formed. Each company had about 90 personnel. In 1815 there were only nine companies, plus one of Young Guard.

An Equipment Train was raised in March 1807 to deal with field maintenance and repair. At first of eight battalions, each of four companies, each of 93 personnel, it was increased to 22 battalions by 1812. There were about 152 draught animals and 34 wagons to a company, plus a forge and an ammunition wagon; but many companies were permanently under-equipped due to shortages. A Guard Equipment Battalion was raised in 1812 and consisted of three companies totalling over 800 personnel with 1,200 horses and 270 wagons.

The ratio of guns to men had been 2:1,000 in 1804, and with the increase of the artillery establishment this had risen slowly to 3:1,000 in 1807–09. The reintroduction of battalion guns in 1809 had brought the figure to 3.5:1,000, and Napoleon aimed for 5:1,000 by 1813, but this was never achieved due to the losses of 1812. In fact the French artillery was often outnumbered by that of the enemy, for example at Eylau, where the Russian guns outnumbered the French by two to one, and at Leipzig, where although Napoleon had 600 guns (1:300) the Allies fielded 900.

Prussia

The Prussian army was organized according to the 1792 regulations, with the artillery scattered amongst the infantry, each battalion having one 6pdr. gun. Attempts to reorganize in 1805 came too late for Jena. During the 1806 campaign there were, however, in addition to the battalion pieces, four regiments of Foot Artillery and one of Horse, each regiment having ten companies. Foot companies had 243 personnel, horse companies had 215. The foot batteries were equipped with six 12pdrs. and two 10pdr. howitzers, the horse batteries with six 6pdrs. and two 7pdr. howitzers.

Battalion guns were abolished under the new

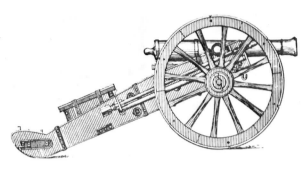

Prussian 6pdr. gun and carriage, with trail chest.

regulations of 1812, and the Prussian auxiliary corps of 1812 was supplied with four foot batteries, each of six 6pdrs. and two 7pdr. howitzers, a half 12pdr. battery with three 12pdrs. and one 10pdr. howitzer, five park and two bridge columns.

In early 1813 Prussia had 1,287 artillery pieces available, of which 93 were 7pdr. howitzers, 81 were 10pdr. howitzers, 271 were 6pdr. guns, and 438 were 12pdr. guns—although many of these, especially the 12pdrs., were fixed fortress guns. In mid-March a figure of 213 *field* pieces is quoted by the General Staff.

By the end of August Prussia had 400 field pieces in 50 batteries: 38 foot batteries (30 with 6pdrs., six with 12pdrs., and one each with 3pdrs. and 7pdr. howitzers) and 12 horse batteries with 6pdrs. (There was also a half-battery of 8pdrs. with the Berlin *Landsturm* and another horse battery with von Lützow's *Freikorps*.) In spring 1813 most infantry brigades had one horse and one foot battery attached, but from autumn that year this was reduced to one 6pdr. foot battery per brigade. Reserve artillery was held at corps level.

The horse batteries were equipped with six 6pdrs. and two 7pdr. howitzers, with their

Prussian 7pdr. howitzer and carriage (very similar to that for the 6pdr. gun) with trail chest.

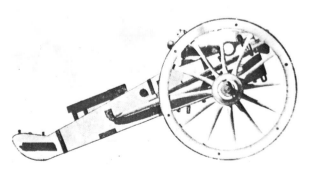

caissons and wagons. The 6pdr. foot batteries had similar equipment, but half the number of caissons. The 12pdr. foot batteries had six 12pdrs. and two 10pdr. howitzers, with their caissons and wagons. In 1813 a special 7pdr. howitzer battery was raised, and this had eight howitzers, 12 caissons and two wagons. There was an all-howitzer battery again in 1814, and five were raised for 1815. Personnel was 155 for horse batteries, 138 for 6pdr. foot batteries, and 203 for 12pdr. foot batteries.

Pack Columns were organized to supply each of the artillery brigades, though in 1813 they often had to supply two or three brigades. These had 135 personnel, 168 draught horses, six each of 6pdr. and 7pdr. howitzer caissons, 12 small arms ammunition wagons, two supply wagons, a tool wagon and a spare parts wagon.

Artisan Columns had 41 personnel, 44 draught animals, three wagons for wheels and timber (four in 1813), and one each for the smithy, fuel, wheelwright and carpenter.

Laboratory Columns, for the preparation of ammunition in the field, had 29 personnel and six wagons. There should have been one per artillery brigade.

Russia

Russian artillery was completely re-equipped in 1805 with 6pdr. and 12pdr. guns and 3pdr., 10pdr. and 20pdr. 'unicorns' or 'licornes'—a howitzer with a flatter trajectory and longer range than other howitzers. (The name was derived from the lifting handles, shaped like leaping unicorns, and the cascable in the form of a unicorn's head, but these decorations appear to have been omitted from the new designs.) This was known as the System of 1805 and incorporated all the latest artillery improvements.

These new weapons were first employed at Austerlitz, where the artillery performed very badly. Investigation revealed defects in the organization and use of the pieces, but no faults in the pieces themselves, and all were therefore retained with the exception of the 3pdr. unicorn, which had been supplied as a battalion piece and was too light to be incorporated into the artillery. It was withdrawn after Friedland in 1807.

Reorganizations during the 1808–10 period

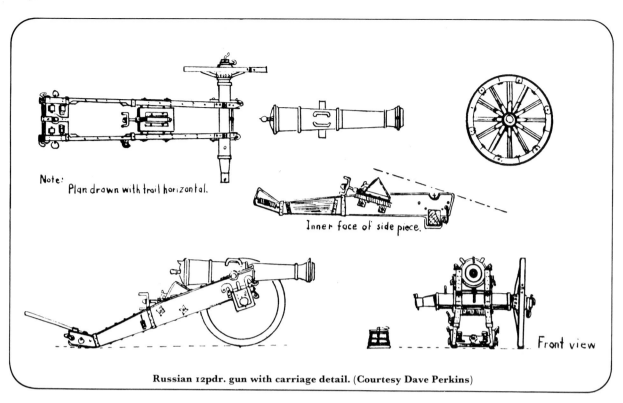

Russian 12pdr. gun with carriage detail. (Courtesy Dave Perkins)

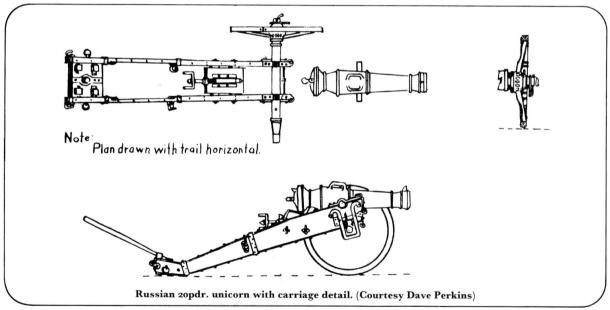

Russian 20pdr. unicorn with carriage detail. (Courtesy Dave Perkins)

provided three types of battery, and this basic organization remained unchanged until the early 1840s. Horse batteries had six 6pdrs. and six 10pdr. howitzers, with a complement of 160 personnel: 'light (position) batteries' had eight 6pdrs. and four 10pdr. howitzers or six of each, with 160 personnel: and 'heavy (position) batteries' had four 12pdrs., four 6pdrs., and four 20pdr. howitzers, with 240 personnel. The howitzers used by the horse batteries were of smaller dimensions and therefore lighter than the foot artillery models. Each piece in every battery was supplied by three caissons.

In 1808 there were 139 batteries with 1,550 pieces, increased to 161 batteries with 1,699 pieces by 1812. Of these 161 batteries 44 were heavy, 58 light, and 22 horse. The others were siege or depot batteries. There were also two heavy, two light and four horse batteries of the Guard, and some light (possibly 3pdr. galloper guns) batteries incorporated in some Cossack hosts. There is little information about these Cossack batteries and we know only that the 'Don Horse Artillery' had 12 guns at Friedland, and there were 12 Cossack guns at Leipzig. Sir Robert Wilson, writing of the 1806–07 campaigns in Poland, says: 'The Cossaque artillery, worked by the Cossaques, which is a late institution, consisted of 24 pieces, extremely light, and the carriages were fashioned with a care and nicety which did great credit to Russian workmanship.'

The field batteries were formed into brigades in 1811–12, creating 27 field brigades, usually of one heavy and two light batteries. It was normal for each infantry division to have an artillery brigade attached in the field. Horse batteries were issued singly at approximately one per cavalry division. There were also ten reserve brigades of four batteries each, and four depot brigades of eight batteries each.

Wilson said of the Russian artillery: 'No other army moves with so many guns and with no other army is there a better state of equipment, or more gallantly served.' At Eylau the Russian guns were in a ratio of six to every thousand men, beyond Napoleon's unachieved dream of 5:1,000.

The Plates

A: Russian foot artilleryman, with examples of ammunition types, to scale

The gunner holds a round of 'fixed' canister, i.e. charge and projectile in one piece. Some fixed ammunition was kept ready, but most was made up just prior to battle. Other types of ammunition are:

(a) and (b) Exterior and cutaway of British common shell, secured to a wooden shoe by tin straps, and with a beechwood fuze.
(c) and (d) Exterior and cutaway of British spherical case, or shrapnel, showing a different method of securing the case to the sabot. Note how the bursting charge and projectiles are in contact with the casing.

(e) Two different methods of attaching the sabot to roundshot. (f) A selection of shot gauges—the right hand one is British, the other two Prussian. (g) Prussian common shell—note difference in fuze from British type.
(h) Russian canister for use in gun, showing projectile canister before fixing of charge container. (i) and (j) Two Russian fixed rounds for use in the Shuvalov howitzer, of characteristic stepped cone shape. (i) is canister, shown 'exposed' here, and (j) may be either heavy canister or double-shotted roundshot. (k) Russian roundshot, for Shuvalov howitzer, again with cone-shaped charge container. No sabot is evident in any of the Russian ammunition.

B (top) Loading a Russian 12pdr. gun
The loader pushes a roundshot and its fixed charge into the muzzle, while the rammer waits to ram it home. By the breech, the ventsman has his thumb over the vent to prevent a rush of air fanning any smouldering fragments of the previous charge and causing a premature explosion. Loader and rammer both wear bricoles—hauling ropes attached to crossbelts—for dragging the piece back into position after firing. Left of the breech as viewed, the man with the portfire holds it well clear during loading. Two men fit handspikes, ready for laying the gun, and the NCO looks on.

B (bottom) Priming a Prussian 6pdr. gun
The ventsman has just pricked a hole in the charge container through the vent, and is inserting a firing tube. The man with the portfire stands ready by the breech.

C (top) Aiming an Austrian 3pdr. gun
Final laying of the gun is taking place under the supervision of the NCO in command, while the firer awaits the order to touch portfire to firing tube the moment the handspike man has jumped clear. The crew wear winter uniform; those with blue facings are *Handlanger*, or artillery labourers. This corps was supposed to provide mere muscle, but inevitably some picked up the rudiments of the artilleryman's craft, and helped serve the gun in emergencies.

C (bottom) Running back a French 12pdr. gun
A heavy gun of the Gribeauval system is run back
into position after firing. The crew wear the
campaign uniform of the Foot Artillery of the
Imperial Guard; they have the help of a squad of
Guard Foot Grenadiers. It was normal for
French infantry to be assigned to gun crews as
extra 'muscle' and ammunition numbers.

D (top) Russian 12pdr. gun, limber and six-horse team
*D (middle) French 12pdr. gun, limber and six-horse
 team*
The French method of harnessing was the system
most commonly employed on the Continent at
this date.
*D (bottom) British Royal Horse Artillery 9pdr. gun,
 limber and six-horse team*
Note the double shafts instead of a single-pole
limber, unique to Britain at this late date.

E (top) French pontoon wagon
Two pontoons are carried, the top fitting within
the lower one. Other wagons of this design were
used to carry chesses—the baulks of timber which
were laid on the pontoons to create a bridge.
(Note that for space reasons we have omitted the
front pair of horses of the six-horse team.) Most
countries used this type of pontoon and wagon,
with minor differences. The Russian pontoon was
more rounded at stem and stern and resembled a
boat.
E (bottom) French pontoon bridge under construction
Pairs of pontoons, assembled complete with
bridge sections up-stream, were floated down and
attached in position.

*F (top) Replacing a dismounted Prussian howitzer
 barrel*
Prussian gunners using a gyn to replace on its
carriage the barrel of a 7pdr. howitzer dismounted
by enemy fire in battle. The barrel weighed in the
region of 700lbs.
F (bottom) Changing the wheel of a Prussian 6pdr. gun
Damage such as this was common in battle, and
was one reason why wheel diameters were
standardized; the gun wheel is being replaced by
one taken from a limber. This in its turn will be
replaced by another from an empty caisson or a
spare wheel wagon as soon as conditions allow;
getting the gun back into action is the priority.

G: British RHA 12pdr. rocket carriage
The top view shows the carriage in line of march;
the standard limber was used, drawn by a four-
horse team. The rocket 'car' was of special design;
the one illustrated was for 12pdr. and 18pdr.
rockets, and another of similar construction
accommodated 24pdr. and 32pdr. rockets. The
heavy car carried 40 rounds of 24pdr., and that
illustrated carried 60 rounds of 12pdr. or 50
rounds of 18pdr. rockets. The sticks were carried
in half-lengths in boxes along each side of the car.
The two central seats also served as small storage
boxes. In action two rockets could be fired
simultaneously (ignited by two gunners: four
rockets by four gunners, in the case of the heavy
car) from the iron plate trough. This was mov-
able and could be fired at any angle from parallel
to the ground (at point-blank range) to 45°
without being detached from the car. The middle
view shows the trough in position for ground
firing at two angles. In the foreground the trough
has merely been lifted off the bed of the axle-tree
on which it travelled, and laid on the ground.
Bottom view: here the trough is raised to a high
angle, supported at the front by the 'perch' of
the carriage and kept steady by two iron stays
and by a chain from perch to axle-tree.
*H: Austrian gunner, with examples of tools and acces-
 sories, to scale*
He holds the sponge staff and ramrod, the double-
ended staff with which the piece was swabbed
and the projectile and charge rammed down the
bore. All armies used the same basic design, the
swabber usually being made of sheepskin, and
the dimensions of the staff obviously varying with
the calibre of the piece.
(a) A selection of priming wires, pushed down
the vent to puncture the charge bag for the
insertion of a firing tube, thus making ignition
more certain. The types illustrated are typical of
those used by all nations.
(b) Thumb-stall of leather, worn by the ventsman
to protect himself when serving the hot vent. It
was possible for the leather to burn right through
during the course of an action. (c) Tompion,
inserted in the muzzle to protect the bore when
out of battle. (d) Portfire case of leather, to con-
tain and protect lengths of quick-match or portfire. (e) Water bucket, used when sponging out

the piece; leather buckets were also used. The buckets were suspended under the gun's axle-tree. (f) Portfire cutters, used to trim off the burning end of the match when there was a pause in the firing. The large British example illustrated was normally attached to the right side of the trail, just behind the barrel. The simple spring-loaded hand cutters shown here were also used.

(g) From left to right: a British portfire holder with quick-match inserted; and two British linstocks with slow-match. (h) French linstock for holding the slow-match; the match was lit and the stock was thrust into the ground on the gun position, and portfires were ignited from it throughout an action. (i) Powder scoop, used to measure loose powder before the advent of fixed ammunition, and still used for mortars in the Napoleonic period. (j) Straight and crooked handspikes, for inserting in the iron brackets on the trail and levering to traverse the piece. (k) Wormhead and 'ripper', used to draw faulty charges, and to clean out any residue of cartridge. The examples shown are Prussian, but those of most countries followed the same principles.

Notes sur les planches en couleur

A Artilleur russe tenant une mitraille, avec les types de munitions suivants (à l'échelle): (a) et (b) obus britannique. (c) et (d) *Shrapnel* britannique. (e) Systèmes pour attacher les balles au *sabot*. (f) Jauges pour vérifier la taille des boulets de canon. (g) Obus prussien. (h) Vue d'une mitraille ouverte. (i) Vue d'une mitraille pour un obusier russe. (j) Ceci est probablement une balle double pour un obusier russe. (k) Balle pour un obusier russe.

B (en haut) Les servants d'une pièce en train de charger un canon de douze russe. A côté de la culasse, un homme tient la mèche brûlante bien à l'écart, pendant qu'un autre bouche la lumière afin d'empêcher l'air qui a été aspiré par le refoulement du boulet d'aviver les étincelles qui restent. **(En bas)** L'amorçage d'un canon de six prussien; un homme vient de faire un trou dans la cartouche en toile et est maintenant en train d'introduire un petit tube de poudre dans la cartouche par voie de la lumière.

C (en haut) Dernier pointage d'un canon de trois autrichien. Les hommes à col bleu sont des manoeuvres d'artillerie et ceux à col rouge sont des canonniers. **(en bas)** Artilleurs et grenadiers de la Garde Impériale remettant un canon de douze Gribeauval à sa position originale après le déchargement. Il appartenait normalement aux soldats d'infanterie d'aider les servants d'une pièce dans cette opération.

D (en haut) Canon de douze Russien, avant-train et attelage de six chevaux. **(centre)** Canon de douze français, avant-train et attelage de six chevaux. **(en bas)** Canon de neuf britannique utilisé par la Royal Horse Artillery, avant-train et attelage de six chevaux. La méthode française de harnachement était utilisée par la plupart des pays; le système britannique, à double brancard au lieu d'un arbre simple, était unique à cette époque.

E Haquet à ponton français (la première paire de chevaux a été omise pour des raisons d'espace) et pont de bateaux en construction. Une section de pont en bois était construite sur chaque paire de pontons et lâchée dans l'eau pour suivre le courant et être attachée enfin au bout de la section précédente.

F Des canonniers prussiens en train de mettre en place le canon démonté d'un obusier à l'aide d'une bigue et d'une poulie (en haut); ici, ils remplacent la roue abîmée d'un canon de six par une roue de l'avant-train.

G Affût de lance-amarres de la Royal Horse Artillery. La vue en haut montre l'affût en marche. La vue du centre montre l'auge montée pour le tir et (gros-plan) posée par terre pour tirer à zéro d'élévation. La vue en bas montre l'auge montée pour le tir à très forte élévation, un bout étant appuyé sur l'affût lui-même.

H Canonnier autrichien avec des outils d'artillerie, à l'échelle; les outils utilisés par les diverses nations variaient peu. (a) Piquoir pour piquer un trou dans la cartouche de toile par la lumière du canon. (b) Poucier en cuir pour protéger la main placée sur la lumière chaude. (c) Tampon pour fermer la bouche du canon lorsqu'il était hors de la bataille. (d) Etui pour porter des morceaux de mèche. (e) Seau à eau, utilisé lorsqu'on épongeait le canon. (f) Ciseaux pour couper les bouts de mèche. (g) Etoupille britannique, pour tenir la mèche brûlante et deux boutefeux pour tenir la mèche. (h) Boutefeu français pour mèche à combustion lente; il était piqué dans le sol et les mèches à combustion rapide étaient allumées à sa mèche. (i) Pelle à poudre qui était encore utilisée à cette époque pour mesurer les charges de mortiers. (j) Pics à main—les leviers en bois qui servaient à déplacer la crosse. (k) Des outils pour enlever le débris de la cartouche qui restait dans le canon et pour retirer les charges non tirées. Ceux-ci sont prussiens, mais ceux des autres nations étaient similaires. Le canonnier au centre tient un bâton ayant une éponge à un bout et un écouvillon à l'autre.

Farbtafeln

A Russischer Artillerist, der eine Kartätschengranate in der Hand hält, mit Munitionstypen (massstäblich geschildert): (a) und (b) britische Granate. (c) und (d) Britische *shrapnel*. (e) Methoden der Befestigung einer Kugel am *sabot*. (f) Eichmasse zum Kontrollieren von Kugelgrössen. (g) Preussische Granate. (h) Offene Ansicht russischer Kartätschengranate. (i) Offene Ansicht einer Kartätschengranate für russische Haubitze. (j) Wahrscheinlich eine doppeltgeladene Kugel für russische Haubitze. (k) Kugel für russische Haubitze.

B (oben) Mannschaft beim Laden eines russischen 12-pfünder. Zur Seite neben dem Verschlussstück, und etwas entfernt, steht ein Soldat mit der brennenden Lunte, während ein anderer das Zündloch verstopft, um das Anfachen irgenwelcher übriggebliebener Funken durch den vom Ansetzen der Kugel getriebenen Luftdruck zu vermeiden. **(unten)** Ein preussischer 6-pfünder wird mit Zündpulver versehen; ein Soldat hat eben durch die Tuchpatrone hinabgestochen und führt jetzt eine kurze Tube Zündpulver durch das Zündloch in die Patrone hinein.

C (oben) Das endgültige Zielen eines oesterreichischen 3-pfünder-Geschützes. Die Soldaten mit blauen Kragen sind Artilleriearbeiter und die mit roten Kragen Artilleristen. **(unten)** Artilleristen und Grenadiere der kaiserlichen französischen Garde ziehen eine 12-pfünder-Gribeauval-Kanone nach dem Schiessen auf Stelle zurück. Gewöhnlicherweise waren Infanteristen zugewiesen, den Geschützmannschaften auf diese Weise behilflich zu sein.

D (oben) Russisches 12-pfünder-Geschütz, Protze und 6-Pferde-Gespann. **(mitte)** Französisches 12-pfünder-Geschütz, Protze und 6-Pferde-Gespann. **(unten)** Britisches Royal Horse Artillery 9-pfünder-Geschütz, Protze und 6-Pferde-Gespann. Die französische Spannmethode galt für fast alle Länder; zu dieser Zeit war das britische System mit doppelter statt einfacher Deichsel einzig in seiner Art.

E Französischer Pontonwagen (wegen Platz ist das vorderste Paar Pferde weggelassen worden): Schiffbrücke im Bau. Auf jedem Paar Brückenkahne wurde ein Teil der Holzbrücke gebaut, den man dann stromabwärts schwimmen liess bis er am Ende des vorhergehenden Teils befestigt werden konnte.

F Preussische Artilleristen bringen ein abmontiertes Haubitzerrohr mit Scherenkran und Rolle wieder auf die Lafette; das beschädigte Rad eines 6-pfünder-Geschützes wird mit einem Rad von der Protze ersetzt.

G Raketenlafette der britischen Royal Horse Artillery. Oben sieht man die Lafette marschbereit. In der Mitte wird die Rinne zum abfeuern aufgestellt und (vorne) auf die Erde gelegt um bei Nullerhöhungswinkel abzufeuern. Unten wird die Rinne für Steilfeuer aufgesetzt, wobei ein End in die Lafette selbst gestützt wird.

H Oesterreichischer Artillerist, mit Artilleriewerkzeug (massstäblich geschildert); das Werkzeug der verschiedenen Nationen hat sich nur geringermassen unterschieden. (a) Stecher, um die Tuchpatrone durch das Zündloch des Geschützes durchzustechen. (b) Lederner Däumling zum Schutz der über dem heissen Zündloch gehaltenen Hand. (c) Mündungspropfen, womit die Mündung des Geschützes ausser der Schlacht geschlossen wurde. (d) Hülle zum Tragen abgeschnittener Längen Lunte. (e) Wassereimer, zum Gebrauch beim Auswischen des Rohres. (f) Schneidewerkzeug zum abschneiden der Luntenlängen. (g) Britisches *portfire*, ein Behälter für die brennende Lunte; und zwei *linstocks* (Luntstöcke), Luntenbehälter. (h) Französischer *linstock* für langsam brennende Lunte; er wurde in die Erde gesteckt und die schnellbrennenden Zündschnüre wurden von der glimmenden Lunte angezündet. (i) Pulverschaufel, zu dieser Zeit immer noch im Gebrauch, um die Ladung für Mörser zu messen. (j) Hebenbäumer—die hölzernen Hebel, womit der Lafettenschwanz bewegt wurde. (k) Werkzeug zum Ausputzen von Patronenreste aus dem Rohre und zum Ausziehen unabgefeuerter Ladung. Das sind preussische Werkzeug; die von anderen Nationen sind aber ähnlich gewesen. Der Artillerist in der Mitte hält in der Hand einen doppelten Ladestock mit Schwamm und Ansetzkolben.